FSOT Study Guide

2022-2023

Updated Prep + 462 Test Questions and Detailed Answer Explanations for the Foreign Service Officer Test (Includes 3 Full-Length Practice Exams)

D1695818

Table of Contents

Introduction

What Is the FSOT?

The Foreign Service Officer Test (FSOT) is an evaluation for individuals who desire to be employed as Foreign Service officers. You will need it to undertake a Foreign Service career path, which may be in politics, the consulate or any department of your choice.

The FSOT evaluates your skills, talents and knowledge across various fields, especially as they are related to Foreign Service officers. Everyone can take the online test at special centers around the United States and other countries. You will be allotted three hours to take the test.

When Is the FSOT Taken?

Registration to take the test opens three times every year.

The first registration often comes up January 2 to January 30 if the test will be given between February 2 and February 9 of that year.

Registration comes up every May 2 to May 30 if the test will be given between June 2 and July 9 of that year.

The final registration often comes up every August 29 to September 26 if the test will be given between September 29 and October 6 of that year.

The test is technically free. You will be charged $5, which will be refunded a few weeks after you have taken the test. However, you will be penalized $72 if you fail to take the test after registering. Therefore, avoid registering if you are not sure you will take the exam.

Taking the FSOT

On test day, go to your test center with authorized, nationally recognized identification, such as a driver's license, military ID or state ID. The only acceptable ID for those taking the test at an embassy or consulate is a US passport. Also, remember to take your letter of admission.

Arrive early because you may not be allowed into the center late.

You will have three hours to finish the test. The test is computer based, and you can skip through questions you find difficult and go back to answer them later.

How Will I Be Evaluated?

The FSOT is divided into four parts: the job knowledge section, which has 60 questions; the situational judgment section, which has 75 questions; 65 tests on English expressions; and a written essay. Except for the written essay, the other three sections are multiple-choice questions.

You will receive your score within three weeks of the exam. The pass mark varies from year to year. A total score of at least 154 in the multiple-choice sections is usually required.

The minimum you should score in the essay section is six out of 12 points. If you get as much as 154 in the multiple-choice sections, you will not receive a grade on your essay. Failing to pass the test means you will have to wait another 12 months to take the exam again. Therefore, spend ample time preparing for this test. Studying this guide and practicing the exercises will help you succeed the first time you take it.

What Does the Oral Assessment Entail?

Think of the oral assessment as a job interview. It is meant to see if you have the skills, knowledge and personal characteristics needed for the position you are applying for. To successfully pass the oral assessment:

• Search for oral assessment sessions or attend a webinar.

• Review the 13 aspects of what makes a successful Foreign Service officer. These aspects are:

- Composure
- Cultural adaptability
- Experience and motivation
- Information integration and analysis

- Initiative and leadership
- Judgment
- Objectivity and integrity
- Oral communication
- Planning and organizing
- Resourcefulness
- Working with others
- Written communication
- Quantitative analysis

Which Areas Should I Study When Preparing for the FSOT?

The English expression section tests your mastery and usage of English. You will be examined on aspects of English, such as grammar, idioms, common errors, effective speaking and more.

The sections on job knowledge and situational judgment include topics such as:

- United States government
- United States history, society and culture
- Principles of the United States in international economics and political issues
- World history and geography
- Foreign Service and the laws/legislations of the United States
- Technology—computers and the internet
- Economics
- Mathematics and statistics
- Procedures and methods of administration in the Foreign Service
- Principles of management, human behavior and psychology

How to Score Very High on the FSOT

Everyone who has taken the FSOT will testify that it is a very difficult test. Its questions cover many different subject matters. It is no wonder that only 30% to 50% of those who take the test pass. This book was written to eliminate the complexities and fear that can come with the FSOT.

Most people focus only on the computer-based test and neglect the other areas the FSOT covers. The four major parts of the FSOT include the written test, a narrative test, the oral assessment and security clearance.

Let's explore what each of these parts entails and how to successfully complete them.

1. The Written Test

The written test is computer based, and it asks you a wide variety of general knowledge questions. Expect questions on work experience.

To score high on the written test:

A. Have an idea of current affairs. Be conscious of events all over the world. Listen to the radio. Read the latest news online and in newspapers. Read the *New York Times*, *The Economist* and any relevant material that provides information on world politics, geography, economics, culture, history, etc.

B. Test yourself with the questions in this book. You can also visit other websites, such as sporcle.com, which assess you in a wide range of subjects.

2. The Personal Narrative

You will write this essay after you have passed the written test. In this section, you write an essay on who you are, what you have achieved and the knowledge you have gained over the years. In this essay, you should highlight why you are the best person for the job of a Foreign Service officer. You should portray yourself as qualified enough to be a diplomat.

The essay will be submitted to the Qualifications Evaluation Panel (QEP).

To score high on the personal narrative:

A. Write about any international work or activity you have engaged in. If you have worked abroad or taken an international relations course, highlight this.

B. Be specific about describing your skills or knowledge. State how you have used the required skills of the QEP to facilitate work, study or task efficiency. These qualities include leadership, persistence, effective communication, management skills, etc.

C. Go through the guidelines of the QEP to be sure you are not missing anything.

3. The Oral Assessment

You'll take the oral assessment after you have passed the written and personal narrative tests.

The oral assessment is made of three aspects:

A. A mini-group activity in which you and other candidates are given a task to solve while working as a team.

B. An organized interview, which consists of two assessors and one interviewee. You will provide solutions to hypothetical questions. You will also be asked about your work, study and personal life experience.

C. A writing task on case management. You will have 90 minutes to finish.

To score high on the oral assessment:

A. Practice effective communication and public speaking in front of an audience, because you will be asked to present in front of a group.

B. Have thorough knowledge of the job role of Foreign Service officers. Understand your motivation for wanting to work in the Foreign Service. You can practice this presentation with your friends and family members.

C. Learn how to summarize articles as a form of preparation for the writing task on case management.

4. Medical and Security Clearance

After you have passed the oral assessment, you will have a high-level medical and security investigation. This demands a great deal of paperwork.

Part A: Job Knowledge

Chapter 1: United States Government

The United States is a republic located on the North American continent. It is made of 50 states, 14 independent territories, islands, one federal district and 15 departments. It was founded in July 4, 1776.

The three branches of the US government include the legislature, the executive and the judiciary. The functions and powers of a branch are stated in the acts of Congress.

The Constitution

The US government is neither an authoritarian nor a monarchical government. It practices a democratic system of government, and power among the three branches of government is shared.

The US Constitution is meant to ensure there are proper checks and balances within the three branches of the US government. The Constitution is the pillar that sustains the American government. For instance, it is the duty of the legislature to create laws. However, the executive branch may decide to veto the legislature's bills, while Congress may unite and override the actions of the executive branch. The Supreme Court also has the power to void the laws that the legislature creates.

In another form of checks and balances, it is the duty of the president to nominate judges, who must pass the scrutiny and approval of the Supreme Court—which is the number one judiciary body in the United States.

Each branch of government has its specific function. Let's take a look at these duties:

The Legislative Branch

The legislative branch is also known as the United States Congress. The federal government is bicameral. This means that it is made of two houses: the House of Representatives and the Senate.

The House of Representatives

The House of Representatives is made of 435 seats, and each seat represents a district in the United States. The proportion of representatives per state is based on the state's population. The smallest number of representatives a state can have is one. The representatives serve two years per term. However, there is no limit to how many times a representative can be reelected.

Individuals can run for Congress when they are 25 or older. They must have been US citizens for a minimum of seven years and be able to show evidence of residence in the state they are running to represent.

Aside from the 435 House members who are eligible for voting, there are also six members who do not vote. These additional members are five delegates and one resident commissioner. These delegates are from the following districts: American Samoa, The District of Columbia, the Virgin Islands, the Commonwealth of the Northern Mariana Islands and Guam. The resident commissioner is from Puerto Rico.

The Senate

The Senate is composed of two senators for every state, regardless of each state's population. Therefore, there are 100 senators (two senators per state multiplied by 50 states). An elected senator's term is six years. Almost every two years, about a third of the Senate goes up for election.

What Makes the House of Representatives Different from the Senate?

Although the House of Representatives and Senate are under the legislature, they have different and complementary functions. It is the responsibility of the Senate to approve or consent to the president's appointments. These appointments include federal judges, secretaries of departments, ambassadors and military and naval officers.

The bills for revenue come from the House of Representatives. All legislation must have the consent of both chambers and receive the president's signature before it can become law. The president may veto the bill. If this happens, only a two-thirds majority vote of both chambers can make the bill become law even if the president refuses to sign it.

Impeachment Procedures

Congress is endowed with the constitutional power to impeach federal officers, federal judges and the president. It is a two-step process. First, the House of Representatives has to vote for impeachment. If this process is successful, the Senate will have to vote again for the removal or retainment of the official.

Only three presidents have gone through these impeachment procedures. They are Andrew Johnson, Bill Clinton and Donald Trump, whom the House of Representatives impeached twice. The Senate did not vote to impeach any of these three presidents.

The Procedures of Congress

The provision of Article 1, Section II and the second paragraph of the US Constitution makes it possible for both chambers to create committees for carrying out investigations, drafting of laws and addressing special problems.

As of 2003 to 2005, the 108th Congress had 19 committees in the House of Representatives and 17 committees in the Senate. There were also four committees that combined members from the two chambers. These extra joint committees were in charge of supervising the economy, taxation, Library of Congress and printing. Today, there are over 150 subcommittees in Congress.

The Executive Branch

The President

As of January 20, 2021, the president of the executive branch is Joe Biden, the 46th US president. The vice president is Kamala Harris. She is the 49th vice president of the United States. The establishment and investiture of power upon the executive is seen in Article II of the US Constitution.

In the United States, the president is the commander in chief of the armed forces, the ceremonial head (or head of state) and the chief executive (the head of government).

The president may make diplomatic negotiations and sign treaties. Two-thirds of the Senate must approve these before they are recognized.

The president can pardon offenders of federal laws for everything except impeachment. This pardon can be absolute or conditional, and it can be granted only for offenses against the federal government, not a state government.

If the president is charged with bribery, high crimes or misdemeanors, a two-thirds majority of both houses of Congress is required for impeachment.

The president can adjourn Congress if both houses of the legislative branch fail to decide an adjournment date. This power has never been exercised.

The US Constitution also allows the president the power to convene the House of Representatives and Senate when there is an extraordinary occasion, such as war, nominations and emergency legislation.

The Vice President

After the president, the next highest rank in the federal government is the vice president. According to Article I, Section III, Clause IV-V, the vice president is the president of the Senate. As ex officio, that is a non-elected Senate member. The vice president can cast a vote when there is a tie.

The Cabinet, Departments and Agencies

To enforce and administer federal laws, Congress creates federal executive departments. The president chooses the head of the 15 departments and sends those choices to the Senate for approval. These heads of department form the council of advisers, otherwise known as the president's cabinet.

There are other bodies and staff within the executive branch. This includes the National Security Council, the Council of Economic Advisers, White House staff, the Office of Management and Budget, the Office of the United States, trade representatives, the Office of Science and Technology Policy, the Council on Environmental Quality and the Office of National Drug Control Policy. Workers in these agencies are known as federal civil servants.

The Judicial Branch

The basic function of the judiciary, according to Article III, is to interpret and apply the laws of the US Constitution. It is the role of the judiciary to hear and decide on cases brought before it.

The Supreme Court of the United States

Article III, Section I of the US Constitution, is the basis of the establishment of the Supreme Court. This section of the US Constitution gives Congress the authority to set up other lower courts when necessary. Section I of Article III stipulates no term limits given for judges at federal and state levels. According to Section II of Article II, it is the president's role to appoint a federal judge and the duty of the US Senate to give approval.

According to the 1789 Judiciary Act, the United States is subdivided into judicial districts. Each of these districts has a federal court. The act, which has a three-tier framework, consists of the Supreme Court, 94 district courts, 13 appeals courts and two special jurisdiction courts.

The US Congress possesses the power to remodel or revoke federal courts, which are lesser than the Supreme Court.

When there is a dispute or controversial issues between states, the United States Supreme Court has the responsibility to interpret the law and may declare any law of the legislative branch unconstitutional. Although this power of nullifying laws as unconstitutional (judicial review) is not clearly stated in the US Constitution, Chief Justice Marshall, in Marbury v. Madison in 1803, was the first to declare a judicial review.

The hierarchy of the court puts the Supreme Court as the apex court, followed by the Courts of Appeal and then the United States District Court. The United States District Court is the most common court where federal laws are administered.

There is a provision for judicial independence in the US Constitution. However, the Constitution states that federal judges are recognized and eligible for service only when they display good behavior while in office. It is possible for judges to be impeached, just as the president and other officers are impeached.

Although the legislative branch may decrease the salary of judges in the future, all Article III judges are immune to legislative-induced reduction.

United States Elections

Suffrage, which is the eligibility to vote, has taken a new shape over the years. At the beginning of US history, voting was not a federal affair. It was relegated to the state governments and was only for White men who owned land. Direct voting was commonly restricted to the two houses of the legislature. In contemporary American politics, there is universal suffrage. Individuals who are 18 or older are eligible to vote. There are no voting restrictions due to race, wealth, religion or gender. Only convicted felons are disenfranchised from voting in some states.

District of Columbia

Since May 29, 1961, the District of Columbia has been eligible for participating in elections. However, the US Constitution provides the District of Columbia with limited representation. It is represented in Congress by a non-voting delegate and is subject to taxes.

Puerto Rico

Only federal employees in Puerto Rico pay federal income taxes on income generated in Puerto Rico. Other Puerto Ricans do not pay this tax. Nonetheless, they pay every other tax, such as the FUTA tax, Social Security and Medicare taxes and taxes on gifts and business. They are represented in Congress by a resident commissioner, who is a non-voting delegate.

The State Divisions

The United States is divided into states, then counties (known as parishes in Louisiana and boroughs in Alaska). The regulations that impact the daily lives of US residents are often those of the state government. According to the Tenth Amendment, the federal government is allowed to exercise only those powers that the Constitution has vested upon it. The state governments can impose taxes to raise revenue, but they are not allowed to print currency.

Every state has a written constitution and laws that it abides by. The US Constitution specifically states that there should be a republican government in each state. This creates a variation in laws regarding matters such as health, education, crime, property and many other issues.

The governor is the highest elected official in the state. After the governor comes the lieutenant governor. There is a bicameral legislature in every state except Nebraska. A court system in every state and the judiciary is either elected by the people or appointed, depending on the state's system of government.

US Tribal Government

Native American tribes are regarded as domestic, independent nations, which enjoy sovereignty even if they fall under the jurisdiction of the federal government. They are sometimes not within the bounds of the state government. Tribal governments are free to set up councils and establish a basis for membership.

In New England, there is direct democracy. Some other states, like Massachusetts, Rhode Island and Connecticut, do not have counties with much inherent power. However, some counties have so much power that they can receive taxes and serve as law enforcement agencies.

Chapter 2: United States History, Society and Culture

History of the United States

The history of the area known today as the United States started as far back as 15,000 BC, when the first tribes arrived in North America. There arose a multiplicity of indigenous cultures, some of which had disappeared by the sixteenth century.

The colonization of America by the Europeans began in 1492 when Christopher Columbus arrived on the continent. Different colonies were established around 1600. As of the 1760s, there were a total of 2.5 million occupants on the Atlantic Coast.

The British government defeated France and acquired the territory. They imposed taxes on the occupants. When these taxes were opposed, there were punitive laws meant to abolish self-government. This led to armed conflicts in 1775 in Massachusetts.

In Philadelphia in 1776, there was a Continental Congress, which proclaimed the independence of the United States. General George Washington led the Continental Army in the Revolutionary War, which led to the independence of the colonies. In 1783, participants signed a peace treaty that identified the borders of the nascent nation. A central government was established, but due to its inability to levy taxes and the absence of executive officers, it was not effective. A new constitution was adopted in 1789, and the Bill of Rights was added in 1791. George Washington and Alexander Hamilton were the first president and chief advisor, respectively. In 1803, the US government purchased Louisiana from France and the country's geographic size doubled.

The United States continued to expand toward the Pacific Coast as its population grew. Slavery became an issue that resulted in both political and constitutional struggles.

Slavery north of the Mason-Dixon line ended in 1804. However, due to the need for mass production of cotton, slavery continued in the South.

Abraham Lincoln became the president in 1860 with the intention of abolishing slavery. He was opposed by seven Southern states that decided to form the Confederate States of America.

When a federal property was attacked in 1861, the Civil War began. The war ended when the US government defeated the Confederacy in 1865. Slavery was finally abolished by the Thirteenth Amendment on December 6, 1865. This led to a Reconstruction era, during which voting and legal rights were given to freed slaves.

The national government grew stronger, but it could not sustain a total victory over slavery when White Southern leaders got back in power in the South in 1877. Through the suppression of Black voters, Southern states instituted a strong policy of discrimination. Southern leaders enacted Jim Crow laws, which established White supremacy. Discrimination was aimed against African Americans and poor Whites, and lynching of Blacks was common.

The Twentieth Century

In the twentieth century, the United States rose to become the foremost industrial power in the world. This was a consequence of greater investment in entrepreneurship and the teeming number of immigrants migrating to the nation with skills and knowledge to offer and capital to invest. The construction of railroads, industrial mines and factories also led to the industrialization of American society.

Due to resounding protests against traditional politics, corruption, incompetence and mismanagement, the progressive movement began in the 1890s and lasted into the 1920s. This resulted in various reformations, such as income tax at the federal level, direct voting of senators, women's suffrage and the banning of alcohol.

The civil rights movement had become so popular by the 1960s that there was a social reformation of voting and other forms of sociopolitical discrimination. African Americans and other minority racial groups' right to vote was recognized in the US Constitution.

World War I

At first, the United States took a neutral stance in World War I. Then it declared war against Germany in 1917 and joined the Allies in 1918.

The Great Depression

The United States suffered a crash on Wall Street in 1929, which led to the Great Depression—a period of economic hardship that lasted almost a decade. During this era, President Franklin Roosevelt enacted the New Deal, which supported farmers and established the Social Security program.

World War II

In 1941, when Japan bombed Pearl Harbor, the United States declared war on Japan. It assisted the Allied nations in conquering fascist Italy and Nazi Germany. In 1945 the United States dropped atomic bombs on two cities in Japan, Hiroshima and Nagasaki, ending the war in the Pacific.

The Cold War

A conflict emerged between the United States and the Soviet Union after World War II. The basis of the Cold War was a fight to become the world's first superpower. The battle was indirect. It was seen in space travel, the arms race, propaganda and local wars trying to inhibit the expansion of communism.

The Cold War experienced a sociopolitical death when the Soviet Union dissolved in 1991. After the cessation of the Cold War, much of America's focus shifted to conflicts in the Middle East.

United States Society

US society is a western culture that has its own music, dialect, food, games, lifestyle and literature. The United States has a diversity of ethnicities and races due to widespread immigration throughout its history.

The values of the United States are secular, rational and self-expressive. Due to the country's British colonial roots, Northern Europe is the major influencer of American culture.

The other aspects of American culture come from immigrants from other parts of the world. Historians used to consider the United States a melting pot where other cultures come to integrate as one. However, modern-day historians see the United States as a salad bowl with diversities and pluralism of subcultures.

The culture of US citizens is largely affected by occupation, social class, ethnic background, religion, political ideology and personal orientations.

Social Class Distinction

United States society is made up of class distinctions, although most individuals identify themselves as middle class. Education affects Americans' voting behavior. The elite or educated tend to vote more than the less educated. Those who earn more have access to better health, education and social facilities.

On average, most employed Americans work for 42.9 hours a week. As of 2006, the earnings of an average American were $16.64 per hour.

The races recognized by the US Department of Commerce's Bureau of the Census are Native Americans, also known as American Indians; White or European Americans; Asian Americans; and African Americans. Some argue that Hispanic Americans are a racial group, but the US government categorizes Hispanics as an ethnic group.

About 62% of White Americans are totally or partially of Scottish, Irish, Welsh or English origin. Roughly 14% of White Americans have their roots in Southern and Eastern Europe, while about 86% trace their roots to Northwestern Europe.

African Americans are not the only people who have been discriminated against in American history. Asian Americans have also received their own share of racial discrimination. In 1882 the Chinese Exclusion Act went into effect, banning the immigration of Chinese citizens to America. This act was repealed in 1943. About 120,000 Americans of Japanese descent were jailed in internment camps during World War II. Hispanics have also complained of being fairly and unlawfully treated as second-class citizens.

Segregation led to subcultures in American society, such as Chinatowns, Harlem and the African American society that has produced diverse music genres like rock 'n' roll, jazz, rap and the blues.

Mexican society has impacted the United States with its cuisine, music and the Catholic religion, which is the biggest religious sect in the United States.

In subsequent chapters, we will look at the various sectors of United States society and culture.

United States Tech Culture

Technology is crucial in the lifestyle of the American people. Americans are great consumers of technology because they largely believe that technology is the solution to most of man's daily problems. Examples of new technologies pioneered by Americans include the internet, transistor, lightbulb, personal computer, airplane, video games, online purchases, nuclear power, etc.

Automobiles are widely used in the United States. They are seen as not just luxuries but needs that are essential for private transportation. As of 2001, about 90% of U.S. citizens drove to work.

Alcohol, Smoking and Drugs in the United States

The stance toward alcohol and drugs in the United States has transformed over the years. In the early nineteenth century, alcohol was not prohibited in any way in the United States. However, restrictions started cropping up during the temperance movement at the end of the nineteenth century.

As of 1919, a prohibition law was added to the US Constitution. Prohibition was repealed in 1931.

The trend has moved toward stricter measures against the profligacy of alcohol and drugs since New York enacted tight laws against drunk driving in 1980.

Sports

Baseball is considered the foremost sport in the United States. Basketball, ice hockey and American football are also popular.

For a time, horse racing and boxing captured the American people's attention. However, golf and auto racing have taken over. Tennis is also another popular outdoor activity in the United States.

Food

The United States has a diverse cuisine due to its long history of immigration and diverse ethnic makeup. Americans love Japanese, Thai, Chinese and Italian cuisine, among many more. The type of food an American household consumes largely depends on family background.

Clothing

Predominantly, the choice of clothing in America is informal. Formal wear is mostly used if the occasion is professional. Cultural roots also have an impact on an individual's style of dress.

Levi Strauss, who was a Jewish German and immigrant to the United States, made denim blue jeans very popular in the 1850s. They became popular among many teenage Americans in the twentieth century.

Education in the United States

Education is mandatory at the basic and secondary levels. Governments at the federal, state and local levels oversee public schools.

Students are at liberty to choose public or private school or to opt for homeschooling. Schools are categorized into elementary or primary school, middle school or junior high school and high school. The governing bodies of postsecondary education, or college or university, are separate from the elementary and high school authorities.

Religion

The US Constitution is secular and enforces separation of church and state.

However, Protestant Christianity is the dominating religious sect in the United States. In a 2016 survey, about 74% of Americans are Christians, with 49% Protestant. Twenty-nine percent of Americans identify themselves as Catholics, which makes Catholicism the biggest denomination in the United States. Protestants are subdivided into other smaller denominations, whereas Catholicism is a single unit.

Other religious sects in the United States include Judaism, Islam, Buddhism and Hinduism. About 18% of Americans are not religious. They are atheists and agnostics.

Courtship and Sexuality

Just like in other societies, US couples usually meet through friends, work, relatives or school. Online dating is also becoming increasingly popular.

Another decades-old practice is that of cohabitation, which takes place before or without marriage. Some states have made provisions for domestic partner statutes, which give legal recognition of cohabiting individuals. These states use palimony to financially support one partner if there is a breakup between unmarried couples.

Sex during adolescence is very common. About half of females and about two-thirds of males have had sexual intercourse before adulthood.

Chapter 3: United States Principles in International Economics and Political Issues

United States' principles in international relations are seen in the country's foreign policy. The policy aims to create and maintain a secure, democratic and wealthy world for the good of US citizens and the international community as a whole.

The foreign policy is also meant to control exports, stop the proliferation of nuclear weapons, increase business communication with nations and protect Americans and their investments in other countries.

The power of negotiation and signing of treaties resides with the president. Then it is the role of two-thirds of the Senate to approve.

Unlike in the past, today the United States' economic strength is fast dwindling compared to economic giants like Russia, China and India.

Let's take a look at the economy and other aspects of the US government.

United States Economy and Government

The United States is one of the pioneers of the United Nations and other affiliated agencies, such as the World Bank Group (WBG) and the International Monetary Fund (IMF). Sometimes, the United States has refused to provide financial support to the UN when the country's interests are not recognized.

Apart from these major institutions, the United States also participates economically and as a member in the following organizations:

• World Customs Organization

• World Trade Organization

• Organization of American States

• Group of Seven (G7)

• USMCA, the regional trade bloc with Canada and Mexico

• Asia-Pacific Economic Cooperation (APEC)

• Organisation for Economic Co-operation and Development (OECD)

Nonpartisan in Some Multilateral Discussions

It is not in the foreign policy of the United States to compulsorily participate in all agreements that the international community agrees to and abides by. It does not matter whether the majority of countries in the world are in agreement. If it does not suit the interest of the United States, then the United States is not obligated to support such agreements.

The United States often argues that it will not condone any ratification that will put US citizens as secondary, subject them to unfair treatment, minimize the sovereign powers of the United States or limit its freedom. Some of the international issues that have been debated include political and domestic issues such as climate change, gender relations, gun control, death, a system of government and many other issues. For example:

• The 1920 to 1945 League of Nations Covenant and the Versailles Treaty were signed but not ratified.

• The 1976 International Covenant on Civil and Political Rights was a covenant with heavy reservations.

• The 1976 International Covenant on Economic, Social and Cultural Rights was signed but not ratified.

• The 1978 American Convention on Human Rights

• The 1981 Convention on the Elimination of All Forms of Discrimination against Women was signed but not ratified.

• The 1990 Convention on the Rights of the Child was signed but not ratified.

• The 1994 United Nations Law of the Sea Convention

• The 1996 Comprehensive Test Ban Treaty was signed but not ratified.

- The 1999 Mine Ban Treaty

- The 2002 International Criminal Court

- The 2005-2012 Kyoto Protocol was signed but not ratified.

- The 2006 Non-Compulsory Convention Against Torture

- The 2008 Convention on the Rights of Persons with Disabilities was signed but not ratified.

- The 2014 Arms Trade Treaty

The Hub and Spoke Model and Multilateral Issues

The relationship between the United States and Europe is a multilateral model. An example is NATO. However, the international relationship between the United States and Asia is a hub and spoke model, which uses bilateral agreements between individual nations and the United States.

On May 30, 2009, Robert Gates, then secretary of defense, suggested that Asian nations develop the hub and spoke model while growing other multilateral bodies like APEC and ASPEN. Gates opined in 2011 that the United States has to look at working with indispensable countries to build a multilateral profile.

Oil

A 2014 report shows the United States produces approximately 66% of the oil that it uses. A 2020 report shows that petroleum produced in the United States was more significant than the sum of petroleum exported and consumed. Since the 1990s, the importation rate of petroleum has always been more significant than the percentage of oil the country produces domestically. The discovery of oil resources in the Dakotas and Canada promises a future of freedom from dependence on imported oil.

About two-thirds of the world's oil reserves are believed to be in the Persian Gulf. During World War II, various nations needed petroleum for their military operations. The United States was the foremost oil producer during that period, supplying petroleum to the Allied armies. Some strategists and economists predicted that US oil might eventually be depleted. To avert this, the country tried to establish a good relationship with Saudi Arabia, which had vast oil reserves.

After World War II, the United States continued to protect its interest in the Persian Gulf area during the Cold War. President Jimmy Carter's doctrine was enacted, which was derived from the Eisenhower, Truman and Nixon doctrines. The doctrine made it clear that the United States will use military force to secure its national interest in the Persian Gulf area if necessary.

The president after Carter, Ronald Reagan, continued with the doctrine in 1981. His doctrine stated that the United States would offer protection to Saudi Arabia, which was exposed to threats from the Iran and Iraq war. Some analysts believe that the Carter and Reagan doctrines contributed to the Iraq war in 2003.

Foreign Aid

The United States offers foreign aid to nations and institutions all over the world.

Foreign aid is a key component of the State Department's international relations. As of 2014, the budget for international affairs was $49 billion.

Nonmilitary aid is classified into four areas: humanitarian aid, bilateral development aid, multilateral economic contributions and economic assistance, which is in alliance with US goals.

In 2014, $23 billion in international donations made the United States the world's biggest foreign aid donor. USAID, the US Agency for International Development, is in charge of most of the bilateral economic assistance the United States offers. The Treasury Department provides multilateral assistance. Apart from state-sponsored funding, churches, agencies and philanthropists also offer foreign aid.

Foreign aid in the United States is seen as political. Liberals seem to provide more foreign aid than conservatives.

Military

In 2016, the United States started military attacks on the Islamic State of Iraq, Al-Qaeda and the Levant. It is involved in the Yemen Civil War and the Syrian Civil War.

The naval base at Guantanamo Bay contains what the United States has declared to be unlawful combatants, and this has raised a lot of debate on the national and international politics of the United States.

The US military is also concerned about political and sociocultural stability in Afghanistan and Iraq's governments. It is interested in Russian activities in Ukraine and what Saudi Arabia is doing in Yemen. More currently, the 2021 administration of President Joe Biden has declared the end of military interventions in Afghanistan. Currently, there are debates over the necessity and impact of the reductions in the United States' mediation roles.

Mutual Defense Collaborations

The United States was one of the major pioneers of NATO, which is a collaboration of 29 European and North American nations. NATO was established in the heat of the Cold War to secure Western Europe against the Soviet Union. The NATO treaty compels the United States to fight alongside any nation under NATO when there is an external attack. This agreement is regarded as a mutual defense, where each country within NATO will support members in times of war.

The US government has mutual defense agreements with Japan, New Zealand, Australia, the Philippines, South Korea, Thailand and other countries once in the Southeast Asia Treaty Organization.

The United States is also in a mutual defense agreement with South America, the Caribbean and Central America. This agreement is based on the Inter-American Treaty of Reciprocal Assistance.

The United States takes it upon itself to defend three states under the Compact of Free Association. These states are Palau, the Federated States of Micronesia and the Marshall Islands.

Unilateral and Multilateral Military Operations

Ever since World War II, the United States has held a permanent position in the United Nations Security Council. It also wields veto power. It supplies a relatively minute quantity of personnel to support the UN's peacekeeping actions.

Sometimes, the United States acts not directly on international issues but through NATO. This indirect intervention is seen in NATO's role in attacking Yugoslavia, Afghanistan, Bosnia and Herzegovina. However, the US military often prefers to work unilaterally or through ad hoc coalitions, as seen in the 2003 operations in Iraq.

The United Nations Charter emphasizes that military operations must be for self-defense or with the approval of the United Nations Security Council. Many US operations have flouted this rule. There have been several instances in which the United States and NATO were charged with crimes against international law. An example is seen in the US operations in Yugoslavia in 1999 and Iraq in 2003.

The Exportation of Democracy

There are ongoing studies that seek to identify how successful the United States has been in exporting democracy to other countries. Professor Abraham Lowenthal and other scholars of international relations opine that American efforts to transfer democracy to different parts of the world have mostly been futile. Other analysts and critics assert that US interventions in other countries have resulted in a mixture of outcomes.

US Covert Operations

One US foreign policy is the use of covert operations to displace foreign governments that oppose the interests of the United States. The United States often uses the Central Intelligence Agency (CIA) to carry out its covert operations. The State and Naval Departments are sometimes involved in these covert operations.

Some historical situations in which the United States has successfully toppled foreign governments include the 1953 Iran operation, 1954 covert actions in Guatemala, the Congo in 1960, the 1961 operations in the Dominican Republic, the 1963 South Vietnam operations, Brazil in 1964 and the US role in Chile in 1973. The United States has covertly promoted insurgencies and made assassination attempts when it wanted to protect its interests, including alleged attacks on Fidel Castro of Cuba and interventions in Syria in 1949.

As of 1953, it is alleged that the CIA collaborated with the British government to work against Mohammed Mossadegh, the prime minister of Iran. This action was termed Operation Ajax, and it was carried out because the prime minister wanted to nationalize the production and control of oil. Mohammed Mossadegh's policy was a threat to the business of the Anglo-Persian Oil Company.

The US government, through the CIA, collaborated with the Mossad of Israel to support the government of Iran in setting up the SAVAK intelligence unit, which used torture to bring down opposition parties.

There are many other instances when the United States has covertly played roles in foreign countries for political and economic reasons, which by extension are to protect the interest of the United States.

Chapter 4: World History and Geography

History of North America

A Spanish settlement was established in St. Augustine, Florida, in 1565, followed by Roanoke, a British settlement established by the Plymouth Company in present-day Virginia in 1587. The London Company arrived in 1606 in the area that would become known as Jamestown, Virginia.

The French established Quebec in 1608, and the Dutch established a colony in what is now known as New York in 1609. Native Americans had to contend with new diseases brought by Europeans, as well as the slave trade.

Many people believe Christopher Columbus discovered America, but the landmass was already inhabited before Europeans ever set foot on it. Thousands of years ago, the Beringia land bridge, which once connected Siberia and Alaska, was a common route for early migrants from Asia to the Americas. Some of these indigenous people, referred to as First Nations in Canada or Native Americans in the United States, belonged to small clans or families, while others controlled vast territories or were part of vast empires. Hunting and gathering was a way of life for some groups, but farming was a way of life for many others. An estimated 50 million indigenous people lived in North and South America before European contact.

The impact of European colonization on North American culture cannot be overstated. Spanish and Portuguese colonization of the Americas was sparked in 1492 when Christopher Columbus made contact with the Bahamas, Cuba and Hispaniola. It was Columbus who coined the term "Indian" because he believed he had arrived in the East Indies, which are now known as East and Southeast Asia. Over time, both French and English colonists gained territory and established permanent settlements.

The first indigenous groups to feel the effects of European colonization were those in the east. In order to free up land for European settlement, many Native Americans were forcibly relocated to the interior of North America. The indigenous peoples of the Americas were devastated by disease and war. Invaders from Europe brought smallpox, measles and cholera to North America, which were previously unheard of. Ninety percent of the indigenous population perished in some areas.

Throughout most of the seventeenth and eighteenth centuries, France, the United Kingdom and Spain established colonies in the Americas, and the present-day population of North America has been heavily influenced by these developments. For the most part, the British built their settlements in coastal areas, including the thirteen colonies that would go on to become independent states and lay the foundations for the United States. Much of Canada and the Mississippi River basin was colonized by the French.

The French established a fur trading post in what would later become the city of Quebec. Present-day Florida, as well as much of Central and South America, was colonized by Spain, which extended into what is now the Southwest United States. Spain sought opportunities to spread the Roman Catholic faith to indigenous peoples and acquire valuable resources like gold.

As in present-day North America, the economies of the early British colonies were highly specialized. Commerce thrived, particularly in the Massachusetts Bay area. Tobacco plantations dotted the Chesapeake Bay region of Virginia and Maryland. There were a number of small independent farmer colonies in the Mid-Atlantic region around New York, New Jersey and eastern Pennsylvania. There were large cotton plantations in the Carolinas and further south. Slavery was prevalent on these vast plantations, leaving a dark mark on North America that would last for another 250 years.

Indentured servants were initially employed by the colonists. In order to pay for their journey to the United States, these workers agreed to work for an employer for a set period of time. When their indentured servitude contract expired, these indentured servants were free to work for themselves. Indentured servants accounted for more than half of all European immigrants to the United States prior to the American Revolution.

Indentured servitude was gradually replaced by slavery as indentured servants gained their freedom. First, Portuguese ships brought African slaves to North America in the 1500s. Many nations would participate in transatlantic slave trades later on, with England dominating by the late 1700s. Sugar colonies in the Caribbean and Brazil were the primary destinations for most slaves. A total of 12.5 million Africans are estimated to have been transported to the New World as slaves.

Slaves were employed by the British as domestic servants or laborers in the northern colonies and as farm laborers in the southern colonies. Liberation from slavery was finally achieved through the Civil War, but the practice had been ingrained into American economics for so long, it had to be done by force. The State of Mississippi explained its reasons for leaving the union in its secession statement: "It is only just that we should declare the prominent reasons which have induced our course in the momentous step that our State has taken of dissolving its connection with the government of which we have so long formed a part. Slavery is the world's most important material asset and our position is strongly linked to it."

Contemporary Political/Physical Map of North America

For the most part, North America lies between the Arctic Circle and the Tropic of Cancer, making it the third-largest continent in the world. Lying within 500 miles (800 kilometers) of both the North Pole and the Equator, it extends more than 5,000 miles (8,000 kilometers). It covers a total of 9,355,000 square miles (24,230,000 square kilometers).

The History of South America

Many explorers made long journeys into South America's densely forested interior during the first 30 years of the 1900s. For transportation and commerce, South America relied on waterways, with few roads connecting major cities. Often, the only way to get from one city to another was to travel down a river that meandered through dense tropical rainforests. People who lived along riverbanks were often armed and hostile, making it difficult for travelers to cross. Rapids that were too powerful to cross were also a hindrance in some cases.

For South American countries to become economically stronger in the twentieth century, officials realized the importance of mapping their nations, cutting roads across their vast wildernesses and building cross-country communications systems.

Cândido Mariano da Silva Rondon was one of the greatest explorers in South America. While working for the Brazilian army in 1890 as an engineer, he began exploring the Brazilian interior and the continent's Atlantic coast, eventually leading him to the state of Mato Grosso, where he set out to build a telegraph line and a road to Rio de Janeiro. With those two tasks completed, he took on the daunting task between 1900 and 1906 of building a nationwide telegraph network. Rondon's travels took him to previously unexplored territories.

British army officer Percy Fawcett traveled to South America to survey the border between Bolivia and Brazil as Rondon completed the Brazilian line. To further his exploration of this little-known region, Fawcett returned several times to meet with locals who told him stories of lost cities in the South American interior. He was accompanied by a group of men from a variety of backgrounds, including a waiter, a silversmith and a baker, as he set out to survey the Rio Verde in eastern Bolivia. The group completed the survey despite numerous difficulties, but five of the porters died shortly afterward, probably as a result of the trip's rigors.

After Fawcett's trip to Rio Verde in 1908 and a return trip in 1909, Hiram Bingham set out in 1911 to search for the lost capital of the Incas in the South American wilderness. At its peak in the sixteenth century, Inca rule stretched from the northern border of modern Ecuador to a river in central Chile. It is estimated that the Inca population was approximately 12,000,000 at the time of the Spanish conquest

The Incas had fought a last desperate rebellion against Spanish invaders from the city of Vilcabamba in 1572, and Bingham was searching for the city to retrace the Incas' route through the wilderness. This led him to discover Machu Picchu (the most famous of a series of fortifications, encampments and signal towers along the Incan footpath system) in 1911.

Rondon continued his explorations while Fawcett and Bingham made their discoveries. With Theodore Roosevelt (US president 1901–09), he set out in 1914 to cross the River of Doubt, which he had named several years earlier after discovering it. Many members of the team perished in the South American jungle, as has been the case with other expeditions into the area.

Roosevelt died less than five years after his expedition with Rondon, perhaps due to the lingering effects of his ordeal. However, the team completed its mission and mapped the river, which had only recently been discovered.

Contemporary Political Map of South America

The Isthmus of Panama connects South America to North America, forming the southern half of the American continent. The Humboldt (Peru) Current of the Pacific Ocean is to the west. The Brazil Current of the South Atlantic Ocean is to the east. The Caribbean Sea is to the north, and the Humboldt (Peru) Current is to the south.

There are three plates in South America: the South American Plate, which consists of South America, the Caribbean Plate and the Nazca Plate, which consists of the South Pacific Ocean. At 6.87 million square miles, it is the fourth-largest continent in the world. About 400 million people live in South America (2012).

The South American continent is home to 12 states and one overseas region of France, all of which are independent nations.

History of Europe

Everyone knows the Greek myth of Zeus taking Europa away in the form of a bull. Although Greece is the source of many things, it is not the beginning of Europe. That "rebirth of Europe" should not mislead us into thinking that Europeans today are their geographical heirs, despite the profound influence of classical Greece and Rome on European government, ideas of democracy and the rhetoric of government from the Renaissance to the present day. On the contrary, in order to understand the historical meaning of the term *Europe*, we must recognize that its emergence came about as a result of the collapse of the Roman Empire and its political legacy.

The Roman Empire went through a long period of decline and collapse, as documented by Edward Gibbon and others. Romans gradually replaced imperial structures in the west by establishing their own kingdoms in what they called the barbarian regions. In what is now Istanbul, then known as Byzantium, Constantinople was established in 324 as the new capital of the Roman Empire.

New Rome was established in 330 in Constantinople. It became the "queen city," the center of the known world, which continued to refer to itself as the Roman Empire. Despite the shifting of the capital, it was the Mediterranean that remained the heart of the Empire. In the Mediterranean, the Roman Empire was a major power. North Africa, Sicily and Egypt's Nile Valley served as its granaries. Both Romes relied on them to keep their populations at a healthy level. African coasts produced emperors as frequently as Italian or Adriatic ones.

Tolerance for all religions by Constantine I was a result of the city's move from Rome. Once again, the Christian empire was a Mediterranean one, despite Christianity's rapid spread elsewhere. Among the early desert fathers who inspired monastic life was St. Antony, an Egyptian who spoke Coptic; St. John Chrysostomos, known as the "golden mouth," from Antioch; and St. Augustine, a Latin Christian theologian who was born in Carthage. Alexandria, Antioch, Jerusalem and the two Romes were the great cities of antiquity that inspired this world and its spiritual leaders.

In the eighth century, the Byzantine check on Islamic expansion into the peninsula of Europe from the east marked the beginning of the threefold division of the Mediterranean world. When Charlemagne unified the majority of the European peninsula under his personal rule, aligned himself with the pope and established Aachen (Aix-la-Chappelle) as a permanent capital, the division was finalized between 800 and the end of the first millennium. Alcuin, Charlemagne's York-based adviser, referred to him as *Europa pater* (father of Europe).

History of Asia

Some of the world's earliest civilizations were found in Asia. Islamic civilization and the empires of Sumer, Babylonia, Media and Assyria, as well as Sumerian and Babylonian empires, thrived in Southwest Asia, while ancient India, China and Japan flourished in the east. Nomadic tribes (Huns, Mongols and Turks) in North and Central Asia established great empires and sparked a massive migration westward. In the thirteenth and fourteenth centuries, the Mongols' court was visited by early European explorers, including Marco Polo, who documented his travels in his diary.

After Vasco da Gama set sail for India in 1498, European colonization of Asia began. After crossing Siberia, the Russian Cossacks made it to the Pacific Ocean by 1640. There was a trade competition among India, China and Southeast Asia in the seventeenth century as a result of the establishment of English, French, Dutch and Portuguese trading companies. European powers gained political control over the

Indian subcontinent, then over Southeast and Southwest Asia, by exploiting local conflicts and gaining a technological advantage that arose as a result of the industrial revolution.

Trade between China and Japan was made possible by European pressure. US president Woodrow Wilson's ideology caused many nationalist fronts after World War I and weakened European stature in Asia.

Asia was severely impacted by World War II and the subsequent conflicts. Conflict in international affairs shifted from Europe to Asia as the decolonization process took place along with a rise in Cold War tensions. Asia was rattled by the Arab-Israeli Wars, Korean War and the spread of communism in Vietnam, China and North Korea. Military alliances in the Middle East (the Baghdad Pact, later the Central Treaty Organization) and Southeast Asia (SEATO) were formed in the 1950s to protect against the danger from Soviet and Chinese forces in Asia. The Sino-Soviet rift in the 1960s, on the other hand, ended the possibility of joint Communist-Asian efforts.

Postwar Asia was still dominated by Western powers, such as the United States, Britain, France and the Netherlands, but many Asian nations sought to assert themselves on the global stage. It was the British decision to withdraw from Suez and the United States' defeat in Vietnam that foreshadowed new power relations in the region in the 1960s and 1970s. For a time, China's rising power and the Soviet Union's desire to deepen ties with Asian countries (especially India and the Arab states in the Middle East) created an ideological divide over whether Asian instability was caused by pro- or anticommunist forces.

In the 1970s and 1980s, Asia was also being shaped by other factors. Constant population growth had left many countries in poverty, with inadequate health care, a workforce that was largely underemployed and environmental destruction at an all-time high. Iran and Iraq had a war in which they both invaded each other's territory. Pakistani troops invaded Indian territory. Chinese troops invaded Vietnamese territory, and Indonesian troops invaded Vietnamese territory. The Middle East–led oil embargo crises of 1973–74 and 1979 and the rising economic power of Japan, South Korea, Taiwan, Singapore and Hong Kong shook the old world economic order that had previously been dominated by Europe and the United States. A new force, Islamic fundamentalism, swept to power in Iran in 1979 and threatened secular governments throughout South and Southeast Asia. Fundamentalists gained the upper hand in Afghanistan in the 1990s.

As a result of the collapse of the Soviet Union in 1991, which was in part triggered by its failed invasion of Afghanistan, a new group of independent Asian nations was born in the region's middle. Chinese economic growth in the 1990s outpaced that of Southeast Asian economies during this period, but the latter suffered setbacks in the late 1990s. To put it another way, Indonesia's economic collapse led to greater democracy, as well as calls for independence or autonomy in East Timor, Aceh and Papua in particular. Some Arab-Israeli conflict combatants began to make progress toward peace in the 1990s as well.

History of Africa

Scientists believe Africa was the birthplace of humans. Stone tools were used for hunting and gathering 100,000 years ago. The first inhabitants of Europe arrived from Africa.

Agriculture had reached North Africa by the year 5000 BC. People tended herds of cattle and cultivated fields. The Sahara Desert was not a desert at the time. It was a lush and fertile land. It became drier and drier and eventually became a desert.

In Egypt, writing was first developed around 3,200 years ago. Bronze tools and weapons were produced by the Egyptians. However, the Sahara Desert cut off much of Africa from Egypt and other early civilizations by the time Egyptian civilization arose. Furthermore, the lack of good harbors in Sub-Saharan Africa made sea transportation difficult. Until around 600 BC, African farmers were still using stone tools and weapons, but iron began to spread in North Africa. There was a gradual spread of iron tools and weapons to South Africa by the year AD 500.

When the Phoenicians arrived in Tunisia from what is now Lebanon in 480 BC, they founded Carthage. The Battle of Zama in 202 BC was Carthage's final battle against Rome, in which the Romans prevailed. Rome conquered Carthage in 146 BC and razed it to the ground to expand its empire.

When Nubia and Kush were established, Egypt's influence spread further upriver on the Nile. Sudan, Eritrea and northern Ethiopia all bear the imprint of southern Arabian culture. Civilization had spread to the region by the time of Axum's rule in

AD 50. Axum exchanged goods with Rome, Arabia and India, among others. In the fourth century, Axum became a Christian city.

The Roman Empire, meanwhile, grew. Egypt became part of the Roman Empire in 30 BC In AD 42, Morocco was absorbed. However, the Sahara Desert cut off the rest of Africa from Rome. Egypt was conquered by the Arabs in AD 642. When they conquered Tunis and Carthage between AD 698 and 700, North African coasts were soon under their control. It was only a matter of time before the entire coast of North Africa became Muslim. The Muslims cut off Ethiopia from Europe, but Ethiopia remained Christian.

In northern Africa, kingdoms began to form around AD 800. In the north, they traded with Arabs. As a result, Islam spread to other African countries. Luxury goods and salt were brought by Arab merchants. The Africans gave them gold and slaves in exchange.

Ghana was one of the first African kingdoms. (It included parts of Mali and Mauritania, as well as the modern country of Ghana.) Ghana was known as the land of gold by the ninth century. However, Africans from further north destroyed Ghana in the eleventh century.

In Southwest Nigeria, Ife was the capital of a great kingdom in the eleventh century. Terracotta sculptures and bronze heads were made in Ife in the twelfth century by local craftsmen. However, Ife was in decline by the sixteenth century.

Benin was a third African country. (Benin's medieval kingdom was larger than today's country.) It was a wealthy and powerful country in the thirteenth century. It was also during this time that Mali was established as a sovereign state. Mali was a wealthy and powerful country by the fourteenth century. As a major trading hub, Timbuktu sold salt horses, gold and slaves in addition to other goods.

However, in the sixteenth century, Songhai conquered Mali and destroyed the kingdom. During the fourteenth and fifteenth centuries, Songhai was a kingdom located east of Mali on the Niger River. Around 1500, Songhai was at its most prosperous point. Defeated by the Moroccans in 1591, its kingdom was broken up by the conquest.

Near Lake Chad, the state of Kanem-Bornu was another great North African power. In the ninth century, Kanem-Bornu rose to prominence and remained independent until the nineteenth century. The Arabs, meanwhile, sailed down Africa's east coast. In some cases, they established states like Mogadishu. Zanzibar became their final destination.

Throughout the interior of the continent, some peoples organized themselves into kingdoms. Great Zimbabwe boasted a staggering 1,430 impressive stone structures. During the Middle Ages, Ethiopia was a thriving country. Built in 1200, St. George's Church is one of the country's most famous landmarks.

During this time, the Portuguese were scouting out the African coast. They arrived in the Azores in 1431. In 1445 they arrived at the Congo River's mouth. Portugal finally made it around the Cape of Good Hope in 1488. Europeans began transporting African slaves across the Atlantic as early as the sixteenth century. Slavery, however, was not new to Africa. Over the course of centuries, Africans sold one another as slaves to Arabs.

The transatlantic slave trade grew into a massive industry. Ships from the British Empire transported manufactured goods to Africa in the eighteenth century. They exported slaves to the West Indies and brought sugar back to England from that region (the "Triangular Trade"). A large number of European countries were also involved in the slave trade.

Slave hunting by Europeans was prohibited in the interior. The slaves were instead brought to the coast by Africans. Slaves who were not sold were either killed or sold to other Africans for their own use as slave labor. Meanwhile, Barbary pirates from the North African coast preyed on Spanish and Portuguese ships from the sixteenth through the eighteenth centuries. They also kidnapped slaves from Europe's coasts.

Most of North Africa's coastline was taken over by Turks in the sixteenth century. Egyptians were taken over in 1517, and by 1556, most of the coast of the Mediterranean was theirs. As time went on, the people of South Africa built even more formidable kingdoms. Guns purchased from the Turks helped the Kanem-Bornu Empire grow during the sixteenth century. Although it survived, Ethiopia's power and prominence waned in the sixteenth century.

The Europeans, meanwhile, established their first African colonies. The Dutch established a colony in South Africa in 1652, while the Portuguese established colonies in Angola and Mozambique in the sixteenth century. European countries attempted to stop the slave trade in the nineteenth century. In 1807, the British government outlawed the slave trade. European colonization of Africa took place in the late nineteenth century.

South Africa was taken by the British in 1814 after a long and bloody battle with the Dutch. The French launched an invasion of northern Algeria in 1830. When Europeans carved up Africa in the late nineteenth century, colonization became ingrained in the continent.

Togo and Cameroon were taken by the Germans in 1884. Namibia and Tanzania were taken in 1885. The Democratic Republic of Congo was taken over by Belgium in 1885. Madagascar was taken by the French in 1896. French expansion into northern Africa helped them expand their empire. They seized Morocco in 1912, while Italy seized Libya.

Egypt was taken over by the British in 1914. Liberia and Ethiopia were the only African countries not under European control at the time. Italians invaded Ethiopia in 1896 but were defeated by Ethiopians. Zimbabwe, Zambia, Malawi, Uganda and Kenya were all taken by the British. Egypt was also under British rule. Both Angola and Mozambique are still Portuguese-speaking countries.

In Europe, attitudes toward imperialism began to change in the early twentieth century. In addition, churches in Africa provided schools, and the number of educated Africans grew. Eventually, Africans grew impatient for their freedom. In the late 1950s and early 1960s, the movement for African independence was unstoppable, and most African countries became independent.

Seventeen countries gained independence in 1960 alone. However, it was not until 1975 that Mozambique and Angola gained their independence. Africa began to thrive in the early twenty-first century. Most African economies are expanding at a rapid pace today. African tourism is soaring, and foreign investments are pouring in.

History of Australia

Around 50,000 years ago, the first settlers arrived in what is now Australia. Sea levels were probably lower, land was wetter and animals were larger at this time.

The central dry areas of Australia were not settled until around 25,000 years ago, despite the fact that much of Australia had become populated. Around 10,000 years ago, as the climate improved, the population grew at a faster rate.

Around 300,000 aboriginal people speaking 250 different languages lived in Australia at the time of the British settlement at Sydney Cove. The Europeans took the land as their own when they arrived, as there was no obvious political structure in place. Forcibly expelled from their homes, many indigenous people were killed. Many died as a result of the rapid spread of European diseases among the local population. The destruction of natural habitats was caused by the introduction of feral and domestic animals.

Legislation was passed in the early twentieth century to segregate aborigines. As a result, they were limited in their choices of where they could live and work, and their families were split up. Assimilation became the government's goal following World War II. All of the aborigines' rights were taken away, and attempts were made to "Europeanize" them.

Indigenous people in Canada were given citizenship status in the 1960s after a review of federal law. It was not until 1972 that indigenous people were given back some control over their lands. There is still a long way to go for indigenous people in Australia, but the situation is improving.

Capt. James Cook (1728–1779) led a British expedition to discover Terra Australis Incognita. They arrived in Botany Bay on August 22, 1770. As early as the 1780s, British explorers embarked on large-scale expeditions to discover and colonize new territories along the coast and in the interior of the continent.

On Cook's voyage, naturalist Sir Joseph Banks (1743–1820) suggested that Britain could alleviate prison overcrowding by relocating convicts to New South Wales in the late 1700s. Captain Arthur Philip (1778–1814), who would go on to become the colony's first governor, led the First Fleet as it sailed for Botany Bay in 1787. On

January 26, 1788, the First Fleet arrived in Australia and established the country's first settlement.

Eleven ships, 750 male and female prisoners, four marine companies and two years' worth of supplies made up the fleet. New South Wales was a harsh and inhospitable place for the newcomers, and the colony was under constant threat of starvation for at least 16 years.

Six colonies were established by the British, each with its own set of rules and traditions. These disparities hampered Australia's economic progress. However, the discovery of gold in the 1850s changed the colony's appearance. Increased economic activity and a shift in colonial social structures were the results of the massive influx of newcomers.

As new settlers moved in to farm or mine the land, the indigenous population was displaced. As a result of the poisoning of their food and water supply and the removal of their food resources, this can be categorized as genocide. Aboriginals were systematically being removed from their families by the Australian government as recently as the early 1970s.

The Great Crash of the 1890s in Australia caused high unemployment and many businesses to go bankrupt. Consequently, the formation of a federation was absolutely essential. To keep other nations from taking over land, each of the six colonies agreed to be governed by the same court.

Britain's Commonwealth of Australia was established in the late 1900s. In 1901, Australia became a federal country (although many of the legal and cultural ties with England remained). When Australia became a federal state, it was able to divide its power between national and local levels of government. It was not until Canberra had been completed that Melbourne was chosen as the location of government.

Chapter 5: The Foreign Service and the Laws/Legislations of the United States

The Foreign Service, under the oversight of the US State Department, is the primary structure the US federal government uses to carry out diplomatic functions. It is estimated that there are about 13,000 skilled workers who are enforcing the foreign policies of the United States and supporting citizens of the United States in other countries.

Workers in the Foreign Service also work in the headquarters of any of the four agencies for foreign affairs. These agencies include:

• The Department of State, which has its headquarter at the Harry S Truman Building in Washington, DC

• The Department of Agriculture

• The Department of Commerce

• The US Agency for International Development

The Director General

The director general of the Foreign Service is appointed by the president with the suggestion and approval of the Senate. By tradition, the director general is not handpicked from any other department. The person must have been or currently be a Foreign Service officer. Through the 1946 Foreign Service Act, Congress established the Office of the Foreign Service director general.

Today, the Foreign Service is overseen by director general Carol Perez.

1946 to 1980

From 1946 to 1980, the secretary of state made the appointment of the director general. The first director general of the Foreign Service was Selden Chapin. He was in office for just six months before Christian Ravndal was appointed to replace him. Christian Ravndal stayed in office until 1949.

1975 to 2016

From November 23, 1975, until October 2, 2016, the director general was also declared the director of the Bureau of Human Resources. Being the superintendent of the bureau, the rank of the director general was the same as the assistant secretary of state. Today, both positions are no longer held by the same person.

The position of the director general is not gender-selective. As of 2021, the past four directors general of the Foreign Service have been women.

The first female Foreign Service officer was Lucile Atcherson Curtis. In 1923, she was appointed as a diplomatic officer/consular officer, positions that were later combined in 1924 to become a Foreign Service officer.

The Rogers Act

The Foreign Service was formed in 1924 through the Rogers Act. It was made to be a single administrative unit that combines all diplomatic and consular services as one. The Rogers Act states that the US secretary of state sends diplomats to other nations through the Foreign Service system.

To be selected to serve the United States as a Foreign Service officer, you must pass different written and oral assessments. Foreign Service officers (FSOs) are assigned to one of the 265 US diplomatic bases all over the world. These diplomatic missions include consulates, embassies and other US facilities.

The Rogers Act was also the progenitor of the Board of the Foreign Service, which created the Board of Examiners of the Foreign Service for the administration of Foreign Service examinations.

The Foreign Commerce Service was created in 1927 when Congress gave a diplomatic credential to the Department of Commerce representatives in other nations.

Other legislation was passed in 1930 to establish the Foreign Agricultural Service from the Department of Agriculture. The civil servants working in the agricultural and commercial extensions were diplomats, but they were not Foreign Service officers until the legislation passed.

The 1946 Foreign Service Act

When the Department of State made a request, the US Congress in 1946 passed a Foreign Service act that established six categories of employees:

• Foreign Service officers

• Chiefs of mission

• Foreign Service reservists

• Foreign Service staff

• Consular agents

• Alien personnel, initially called Foreign Service nationals, now known as locally employed staff.

If you are a Foreign Service officer, it is expected that you'll live most of your career life in other nations. You will be commissioned for worldwide service. There are also reserve officers whose careers are mostly in Washington, DC. They may be called up for worldwide service.

Under the 1946 act, the Board of Foreign Service Personnel was replaced with the Board of the Foreign Service. The former was meant to administer the structure of promotions, while the latter was broad in scope because it was in charge of the whole personnel structure.

The 1946 act took a page from the US Army as it started the up-or-out promotion system. This system mandated every Foreign Service officer to rise in rank within a certain period or face compulsory retirement.

The position of the career minister came into existence through the 1946 act. The position was given to the highest-ranking senior officers who were in service. The act also stipulated compulsory retirement age.

The 1980 Foreign Service Act

The 1980 Foreign Service Act is the latest legislative reformation in the system and structure. The 1946 act was not effective, and there was much effort in 1970 to eliminate it.

The Foreign Service Reserve was canceled, and there was the reformation of the personnel system for local staff who carry out nondiplomatic missions across nations. The act also created the Senior Foreign Service, which had a ranking system like the armed forces flag officers. It also established danger pay for officers posted to hostile or life-threatening zones.

When the 1980 act was drafted, the commercial attachés were taken back to the Department of Commerce, even though they were still recognized as Foreign Service officers. The 1980 act also combined the attachés in the Department of Agriculture with the already-employed Foreign Service officers who were in the Department of State, the US Agency for International Development and the US Information Agency.

The Foreign Service Members

In this subsection, we will look at some of the members of the Foreign Service. These include:

• Chiefs of mission. They receive an appointment from the president upon the suggestion and approval of the Senate.

• Ambassadors. They receive an appointment from the president upon the suggestion and approval of the Senate.

• Senior Foreign Service (SFS). They are senior or high-ranking leaders who manage the Foreign Service and carry out its responsibilities. Senior Foreign Service personnel may be specialists or Foreign Service officers. They share the same rank as the military flag or general officers. They receive an appointment from the president upon the suggestion and approval of the Senate.

• Foreign Service officers. Also called generalists, they receive an appointment from the president upon the suggestion and approval of the Senate. They specialize in specific subject areas and carry out the primary duties of the Foreign Service.

• Foreign Service specialists. They contribute special skills and functions that the Foreign Service Department needs to stay productive. These are often IT specialists, special agents of DSS, facility managers or expert nurses. They receive an appointment from the secretary of state.

• Foreign Service nationals (FSNs). Their duties are administrative, technical, clerical, fiscal and more across various countries. They may be natives of the country and were once called third-country nationals (TCNs). According to the Foreign Service Act, they are also regarded as members of the Foreign Service and not locally employed staff (LE staff), who may be Americans living in other countries.

• Consular agents. They are in charge of consular duties and other services that the secretary of state assigns to them in foreign places where no foreign post exists.

• Diplomats in residence. They are senior-ranking officers who recruit new officers for the Foreign Service. They are found in assigned locations and given honorary positions in universities in the locality.

Agencies in the Foreign Affairs Department

Workers in the Department of State occupy most positions of the Foreign Service. The 1980 Foreign Service Act gives other agencies of the US government the liberty to use the Foreign Service personnel structure in positions that require the execution of duties across countries in the world. These agencies/departments include:

• The Department of Commerce, which is also the Foreign Commercial Service

• The Department of Agriculture, which is also the Foreign Agricultural Service

• The USAID

Senior Foreign Service officers of USAID, the Department of Agriculture and the Department of Commerce may be promoted to work as ambassadors, even if the status of career ambassador is mostly from the Department of State.

Terms and Conditions for Foreign Service Officers

It is expected that Foreign Service officers will work abroad at consulates and embassies in different countries. The maximum duration of domestic appointments is six years. However, there can be extensions, such as medical exemptions, to give children the opportunity to finish up high school and other reasons. Not many serve up to the overall limit of eight years, which is for those who are vital to service and those who are serving at the deputy assistant secretary level.

If a Foreign Service officer works domestically for ten years, US law states that the person must then travel abroad. Some officers do not wish to serve abroad because of family life.

The Life of a Foreign Service Officer

Foreign Service officers often have to take dependent family members to their designated place of assignment. But when the area is marked with crises and conflicts, this becomes risky.

Foreign Service Officers' Families

Foreign Service officers' children are affected by the career path their parents have chosen. Generally, Foreign Service officers and their families benefit from exploring the cultures, arts and societies of various parts of the world.

One disadvantage of working as a Foreign Service officer is being exposed to tropical diseases and living in nations beset by civil hostility, warfare and a lack of health facilities. US embassies have been attacked in different parts of the world, including Nairobi, Baghdad, Beirut, Belgrade, Kabul, Dar es Salaam, Islamabad, Benghazi and many others. Lack of public infrastructure, fires, natural disasters and other situational factors are potential risks of working as a Foreign Service officer abroad.

The Posting of a Foreign Service Officer

Generally, Foreign Service officers can, to an extent, determine the area of the world they will be posted to. Nonetheless, barriers, such as language proficiency, rank and place of a previous assignment, may affect an officer's next place of assignment. Selections are made because of what is needed in the Foreign Service. To conform to diplomatic demands, there have been cases of direct assignment to individual posts. Sometimes, Foreign Service officers have willingly chosen to serve in a hostile environment like Afghanistan or Iraq.

To help Foreign Service officers deal with the challenges of being diplomats, the Department of State manages the Family Liaison Office. It helps resolve issues within nuclear and extended families that may be burdensome to a Foreign Service officer sent to a dangerous area.

Clientitis is also known as *localitis* or *clientism*. It is a situation in which the resident staff tends to call the officials and citizens of the host country by the term *clients*. This is seen in businesses and governments all over the world. It is synonymous with *going native*.

An example of a clientitis situation is when a Foreign Service officer assigned to serve at a US embassy in another country protects the interest of the foreign country's government instead of the interests of the United States.

To avoid clientitis, the Department of State trains new ambassadors carefully. The Department of State also reassigns Foreign Service officers after two to three years of serving on foreign soil. When President Nixon was in power, Foreign Service officers were assigned to places, rather than fields of specialty.

The problem of clientitis is most prevalent among diplomats serving in the Middle East because they stay in the locality for a long time.

The Career Structure of the Foreign Service

The Selection Board

Positions in the Foreign Service are highly competitive. Personnel are promoted after their performance has been compared in the yearly Selection Board. In accordance with the Foreign Service Act, every agency of foreign affairs sets up time in service (TIS) and time in class (TIC) protocols for personnel. There is a 27-year limit of commissioned service for officers who do not rise to the position of Senior Foreign Service officer. And there are 15 years of maximum service for officers in any rank who have not attained the rank of Senior Foreign Service officer.

The Selection Board also recommends those who should be selected out of the system because of their inability to work to the panel's standard. This up-or-out system helps keep officers on their toes. It also encourages officers to want to accept challenging and risky assignments.

FSO Career Paths/Tracks

Department of State Foreign Service officers are categorized into five career specialties, or tracks, known as *cones*. These career tracks are consular officers, management officers, economic officers, political officers and public diplomacy officers.

• Consular officers: They are in charge of the welfare of US citizens in other countries. Their role is managing situations, such as adoptions or disasters in the region.

• Management officers: They are in charge of managing the logistics of the consulate or embassy. They prepare and have access to embassy budgets.

• Economic officers: These officers liaise with economic agencies all over the world. They are in charge of foreign policies and collaborations with nations to initiate economic growth and development.

• Political officers: They diplomatically negotiate with a foreign government on political matters.

• Public diplomacy officers: They disseminate information to citizens on the embassy's activities, educational news and press releases.

Chapter 6: Technology: Computers and the Internet

In this chapter, we will explore computers and other aspects of technology. Expect to see questions on computers and the internet in your FSOT exam.

What Is a Computer?

A computer is any electronic machine that accepts and processes data, then produces information. A computer is programmed to automatically work out logical operations.

A complete computer system includes hardware, software or operating system and peripheral tools. A computer may function in a unit or as a network.

We can find computerized systems in almost every aspect of our modern world for both industrial and domestic use. Computerized systems are as basic as remote controls and as complex as special-purpose robots. And have you ever considered your smartphone as a computer? If you have not, you should.

Parts of a Computer

Computers are often classified into hardware, software and peripheral units.

Hardware

This includes all the tangible parts of a computer. They are the parts we can touch. This includes a motherboard, circuits, cables, computer chips, graphics cards, keyboards, sound cards, printers, displays and memory (RAM).

A computer that serves general use has four main parts—the arithmetic logic unit (ALU), the input and output devices, the memory and the control unit. These parts are interconnected.

I. Arithmetic logic unit (ALU)

The ALU helps the computer perform arithmetic and logical operations. These operations include addition, subtraction, multiplication, division, square roots, sine, etc. It assists in solving complex mathematical problems at a faster speed.

II. Input devices

The input devices are used to send data to the computer. The CPU does the processing of the data before it is passed as information through the output device. Examples of input devices include a keyboard, mouse, image scanner, camera, joystick, light pen, touch screen, microphone and trackball.

III. Output devices

Output devices produce information after the input device has sent data for the CPU to process. Examples of input devices are a monitor, printer, video card, projector and speaker.

IV. Memory

Computer memory is a set of cells where numbers are inserted and read. Anything can be represented and stored as information in the memory, including numbers and letters. The memory sees this information only as a set of numbers.

V. Control unit

Also called the control system, this organizes or manages the other parts of a computer. It interprets a program's instructions, then changes them into control signals, which activate other components of the computer system. The ALU, the control unit and registers collectively form the central processing unit (CPU).

Software

Software includes all the intangible components of the computer. Examples are protocols, programs, data, etc. Software consists of computer-encoded instructions or information, such as libraries, computer programs, digital media, or online documentation.

Software is classified into system and application software. System software includes Unix, BSD, Linux, DOS, Mackintosh operating system and Microsoft Windows. Application software includes database management, desktop publishing, spreadsheet, internet access, graphics, audio and games.

Word Processor (WP)

Word processors are software. A word processor functions as a text editor. An example is Microsoft Word.

Desktop Publishing

Desktop publishing is the use of specific software to create documents on a computer with text and images. It helps businesses and individuals publish materials, such as brochures, books, flyers and magazines. When you use desktop publishing software to create content, you have control over the typography, design and layout.

The knowledge and software used in producing books, flyers and other paper materials are also used in creating graphics for infographics, business cards, brochures, presentations, outdoor signs and retail package designs.

Spreadsheets

A spreadsheet is a computer software–generated document that organizes, analyzes and stores data in tabular form. Spreadsheets were invented to make paper worksheets computerized or digital. The spreadsheet application tabulates the data that has been inputted into the cells.

Databases

A database is the organized and systematic collection of data that is stored in the computer system. A database management system, or DBMS, is an application that interacts with users, other applications and the database to collect, analyze and compute data for further use.

The Internet

This is the interconnection of computer networks and devices for communication and the sharing of data. The internet makes use of the IP (Internet Protocol) Suite for internetwork communication across the globe. The internet includes businesses, academic institutions and organizations in the private and public sectors. It transmits a wide range of services and resources, like telephony, hypertext documents, file sharing, electronic mail and world wide web (WWW) applications.

The Origins of the Internet

The internet goes as far back as the 1960s, when the US Department of Defense launched the establishment of packed switching and research to assist computers in time-sharing. In the 1970s, ARPANET interconnected most academic institutions and military networks at the regional level.

The internet has created substitutes for a large number of communication media, such as radio, telephones and paper mail. We now use the internet to publish books, read online newspapers, watch online television stations and blog opinions. It is also a means of socialization and interaction. Businesses are taking advantage of an online presence by establishing online shops.

The internet's management is neither singular nor centralized. The rules of usage and access are not universal. Nonetheless, the IP address and Domain Name System (DNS) are controlled by the Internet Corporation for Assigned Numbers (ICANN) and Names, which is the organization in charge of controlling these spaces.

Internet Protocol

The Internet Protocol allows networks to interact with one other.

IP Address

An IP Address is used for locating users on the internet. They are like home addresses, which have a number and the street of a home or building. When users want to access a website, they input the domain name (such as www.forbes.com) and not the IP address, which is more difficult to remember. The Domain Name System (DNS) converts the domain names into IP, which is more effective.

World Wide Web

The World Wide Web (WWW) is the collection of images, applications, documents, multimedia and other items that are connected through hyperlinks and are visited through URLs (Uniform Resource Locators). These URLs help in identifying web servers, documents, services, databases and other resources.

Hypertext Transfer Protocol (HTTP) is the web's core access protocol. It is also useful in establishing communication between software. Through HTTP, the web can also transfer data and logistics.

The WWW needs browser software to have access to web pages through hyperlinks. Examples of browser software include Mozilla Firefox, Google Chrome, Opera, Safari, Explorer, etc. When searching for information, internet users can make use of search engines such as Google, Bing and Yahoo! Vast amounts of information are now accessible to everyone at any time and from anywhere.

Internet Marketing

The internet is not just a place where people socialize. It is now a lucrative platform for advertising and e-commerce. Digital marketing involves the use of the online space to promote goods and services that are targeted at consumers. It includes social media marketing, email advertising, web banner advertising, search engine marketing and mobile advertising.

File Sharing or Data Transfer

This is the transfer of large data via the internet. Files can be sent to other partners and friends via email attachments. Another way of transferring data is to upload files on an FTP/File Transfer Protocol server where others can download. It can also be uploaded on a website.

Streaming Media

This is the transmission of digital media in real time for consumption by an audience. This includes internet feeds of videos and audio that were produced live. It has features such as previewing and replaying. Because of online streaming media, broadcasting is no longer exclusive to licensed television and radio broadcasters.

Chapter 7: Mathematics and Statistics

The FSOT includes mathematics questions. You will be given practical questions that test your understanding of basic arithmetic problems. Expect general mathematics, such as fractions, simple and compound interest, ratios and percentages and algebra. Let's take a look at the core areas you will be tested on.

Fractions

A fraction can be defined as a part of a whole number. Except for mixed fractions, a fraction often has two aspects: the numerator and the denominator.

The numerator is above the denominator and is separated by a line. For example, 2/3 means that two pieces were considered out of a total of three equal parts.

An easy way to recall fractions is to refer to the line that separates each number as "out of." So a fraction written as 3/5 simply refers to three out of five equal sections.

Types of Fractions

There are three types of fractions—proper fractions, improper fractions and mixed numbers.

• Proper fractions have a higher numerator than the denominator. Examples are 3/7, 6/8 and 11/35.

• Improper fractions have a lower numerator than the denominator. Examples are 7/3, 8/6 and 35/11.

• Mixed numbers are a combination of a whole number and a proper fraction. Examples are $5\frac{3}{4}$ and $6\frac{7}{8}$.

For calculation purposes, you can convert a mixed number to an improper fraction by multiplying the denominator by the whole number, then adding the result to the numerator. The denominator is still represented after the multiplication and addition. For example:

$5\frac{3}{4}$ = 5 × 4 (denominator) = 20 + 3 (numerator) = 23/4.

The Simplification of Fractions

Simplification is simply representing a fraction in its barest form. For example, referring to something as 4/6 is not as easy as 2/3.

To simplify a fraction, divide the numerator and denominator by the same numbers that are bigger than 1. For example, 20/100:

Divide both parts by 2 = 10/50

Divide both parts by 2 = 5/25

Since 3 or 4 cannot divide both sides, use 5 to divide: 1/5.

Addition of Fractions

The easiest way to add fractions is to make the denominators the same. Then add the numerators.

Example 1:

1/4 + 1/4 = 2/4 (or 1/2 after simplifying).

Example 2:

1/7 + 1/14 =

To make the denominators the same, multiply the numerator and denominator of 1/7 by 2 =

2×1/2×7 = 2/14

Therefore, 2/14 + 1/14 = 3/14

Example 3:

A football team won three out of the first five games. Then they won all of the outstanding six games. What fraction did the team win?

Step 1: 3 out of 6 games = 3/6

Step 2: The remaining set is 3. Since they won all, it is 3/3.

Therefore: 3/6 + 3/3 =

Step 3: Make the denominators alike: 3/6 + (2 × 3/2 × 3) = 3/6 + 6/6 = 9/6

Step 4: Simplify 9/6 by dividing both sides by 3 = 3/2

You can either leave the answer as an improper fraction (3/2) or convert the improper fraction to a mixed number:

3/2 is 1 remainder 1. Therefore, the totality is 1½.

Subtraction of Fractions

The subtraction of fractions is similar to the addition of fractions. Make the denominators the same, subtract, then simplify if needed.

Example 1:

4/5 − 1/15 =

3 × 4/ 3 × 5 = 12/15

12/15 − 1/15 = 11/15

Example 2:

There were 6 Foreign Service officers in an office of 12 executives. Then 3 military personnel were taken from the office. What fraction of the office are the Foreign Service officers?

Step 1: 6 Foreign Service officers in an office of 12 = 6/12

Step 2: 3 military personnel taken away = -3/12

Therefore:

Step 3: 6/12 − 3/12 = 9/12

Step 4: Simplify 9/12 by dividing both parts by 3 = 3/4.

Multiplication of Fractions

To multiply fractions, multiply the top and bottom numbers with the given numbers. An example is seen below:

$2/7 \times 2/7 =$

$2 \times 2/ 7 \times 7 =$

$4/49$

Division of Fractions

When dividing fractions, turn the second fraction upside down. Then you multiply. An example is seen below:

$1/2 \div 1/4 =$

$1/2 \times 4/1 =$

$1 \times 4/ 2 \times 1 = 4/2$

Divide the top and bottom by 2

$= 2/1 = 2.$

Arrangement of Fractions

1. If the denominators of a fraction are the same, then the fraction that has a higher numerator is the biggest. An example is:

$5/4 > 3/4 > 1/4$

2. If the numerators of two fractions are the same, then the fraction that has the seemingly lesser denominator is bigger. An example is:

$8/1 > 8/2 > 8/3$

Ratio

Ratio compares two or more things in size or number. You may have come across ratios in cooking, money conversion or scaling while drawing. An example of a ratio is 2:1, 2 to 1, or 2/1.

For example, in a map, the ratio of 1:500 cm means that every 1 cm on the map means 500 cm in real life. Sometimes the antecedent (first number) and the consequent (second number) may be different units; you then need to convert both units to become similar before you start any calculation.

Here are various ways for calculating the ratio:

Example 1: Conversion to a ratio

A bag of 40 candies includes 16 red candies and 24 blue candies. What is the ratio of red to blue candies?

Answer:

16 red : 24 blue = 16:24

Divide the antecedent and consequent by the highest common factor, which is 8.

Therefore,

16 divided by 8 = 2

24 divided by 8 = 3

Therefore the ratio of red to blue candies is 2:3.

Example 2: Conversion of ratios that have different units

Simplify the scale of 3 cm: 15 m in ratio.

Answer:

First, make the antecedent and consequent the same unit (cm is preferable because it is better if both are in whole numbers).

1 m = 100 cm

Therefore 15 m = 1,500 cm.

The ratio would be 3 cm : 1,500 cm

To simplify, divide both sides by the highest common factor, which is 3. Then you will have 1 cm : 500 cm.

Example 3: Ratio in Division

Jimmy and Jones have to share 200 apples in the ratio of 2:3. How many will each of them receive?

Answer:

The apples will be shared equally as 2 + 3 = 5 portions. This means every time Jimmy gets two apples, Jones will get three apples.

Therefore, divide 200 by 5 portions and get 40.

To know what each person will get, multiply both sides by 40.

Jimmy = 2 × 40 = 80 apples

Jones = 3 × 40 = 120 apples

In other words, Jimmy will get 80 apples while Jones will get 120.

Example 4: Scaling in Ratio

Grace is preparing pancakes for six friends but only has available ingredients for two people (50 g flour, 200 ml milk and 2 big eggs). How many more ingredients will she need to make breakfast for six people?

Answer:

The ratio of the ingredients is 50:200:2.

Since you are increasing the quantity from two people to six people, the ratio would be on a scale of 6/2 = 3.

Multiply each of the ingredients by 3:

50 g flour × 3 = 150

200 ml milk × 3 = 600

2 large eggs × 3 = 6

Therefore, an increase to six people will demand 150 g of flour, 600 ml of milk and six large eggs.

Percentage

Percentage is an aspect of mathematics that we cannot escape in our everyday lives. We apply the knowledge in the office, field, school, hospital, store and almost everywhere else. You should expect questions on percentages in your FSOT.

What Is Percentage and How to Calculate It?

Percentage means *per hundred*. It is represented as /100 or % (50/100 or 50%). You may be asked to convert a decimal or fraction to a percentage. Simply multiply by 100 if you want to convert decimal numbers to percentages.

Example 1:

Convert 0.56 to a percentage.

Answer:

0.56 = 0.56 × 100 = 56%

However, 56/100 = 0.56%

Example 2:

If you are planning on saving 20 percent of your income, which is $1,000, for the next three months, how much will you save?

Answer:

20/100 × $1000

0.2 × $1,000 = $200

You will save $200 monthly.

Standard Form

Standard form is a mathematical way of easily representing large or small numbers. Examples include:

1. 10^3 = 10 × 10 × 10 = 1,000

2. 5 × 10^3 = 10 × 10 × 10 × 10 × 10 = 5,000

3. 4560 000 000 = 4.5 × 10^9 (That is 10 raised to the power of 9.)

It is 10^9 because the decimal points were moved nine places to the back.

4. 0.000 078 = 7.8 × 10^-5 (That is 10 raised to the power of -5.)

It is 10^-5 because the decimal points have been moved five places to the right.

5. If A is 6 × 10^6 and B is 5 × 10^3, A × B will be:

First, multiply the two whole numbers:

6 × 5 = 30

Then 10^6 × 10^3 = 10^9

= 30 × 10^9

However, in standard form, the first part (30) should not be more than 1 – 10. Therefore,

$3 \times 10 \times 10^9 = 3 \times 10^{10}$

Simple and Compound Interest

Interest is the extra amount a borrower pays to the lender of a loan. The interest rate is often fixed, and it can be simple or compound.

Simple Interest

It is calculated on the fixed principal rate of a deposit or loan.

Simple interest is calculated using this formula: $P \times r \times n$

- P is the principal amount.
- r is the rate of annual interest.
- n is the term of the loan per annum.

Example 1: Here is a practical illustration of the calculation of simple interest.

To invest in a business opportunity, an investor takes a simple interest loan of $15,000 that has a yearly interest rate of 5%. The investor pays back the loan after four years. What is the sum paid?

Answer:

Simple interest = $P \times r \times n$

= $15,000 $\times$ 5/100 $\times$ 4

= $3,000

The sum paid is:

Interest + principal loan

= $3,000 + $15,000

= $18,000

Compound Interest

Compound interest is the accrual or accumulation of past interest. When the money is not paid at the end of the year, the interest continues to compound.

The formula for calculating the compound interest is:

$P \times (1 + r) t - P$

P = Principal

r = Rate of annual interest

t = The number of years in which interest is applicable.

But you can use a step-by-step method using the simple interest formula and accruing the interest.

Example 2: Here is a practical illustration of the calculation of compound interest.

You are lending $2,000 at a 5% interest rate to a friend over three years. What is the sum paid after the compounding of interest?

Answer:

First year = $P \times r \times t$

P= $2,000; r = 5%; t = 1

= $2,000 $\times$ 0.05 $\times$ 1

I = $100

Second year = $A \times r \times t$

A = I + P = $100 + $2,000 = $2,100

r = 5% = 0.05

t = 1

= $2,100 × 0.05 × 1

I = $105

For the third year, the interest of the second year will be added to the new principal.

Second year = A × r × t

A = I + P = $105 + $2,100 = $2,205

r = 5% = 0.05

t = 1

I = $2,205 × 0.05 × 1

I = $110.25

The sum paid after the compounding of interests for three years is $2,205 + 110.25 = $2,315.25

Algebra

Algebra is an equation that consists of numbers and letters. It involves the search for unknown numbers.

Example 1:

X + 4 = 10. Find X.

Answer:

Take the constant term at the left side, + 4, to the right-hand side (and it changes to -4).

Therefore, we will have:

X = 10 − 4

X = 6

You can also solve this equation by eliminating both sides by 4 (so as to make X stand alone). That is:

X + 4 − 4 = 10 − 4

X = 6

Example 2:

7 − X = 24. Find X

Answer:

Subtract 7 from both sides so as to make X stand alone.

-X = 24 − 7

-X = 17

Since we are looking for X, not -X, divide both sides by -1. Hence:

-X/-1 = 17/-1

X = -17

Example 3:

6X = 12. Find X.

Answer:

Divide both sides by 6 so that X will stand alone.

6X/6 = 12/6

X = 2

Example 4:

Equation 1: $X - Y = 20$

Equation 2: $X + Y = 30$

Find X and Y.

In this problem, there are two equations and two unknown variables. We can use either the substitution or elimination method to solve this problem. Let's take a look at the substitution method.

Substitution Method

When solving with the substitution method, you solve for one of the equations and get the value of any of the variables, then substitute it in the second equation.

Let's use the first equation:

$X - Y = 20$

$X = 20 + Y$

Then substitute this value of X in equation 2. That is:

$X + Y = 30$

$(20 + Y) + Y = 30$

$20 + 2Y = 30$

Isolate 2Y and subtract 20 from both sides.

$2Y = 30 - 20$

$2Y = 10$

Isolate Y by dividing both sides by 2.

$2Y/2 = 10/2$

$Y = 5$

Since we have Y, the next thing to do is to put the value of Y into any of the equations. Hence:

X + Y = 30 will become:

X + 5 = 30

Isolate X by subtracting 5 from both sides.

X + 5 − 5 = 30 − 5

X = 25

Therefore, X = 25 and Y = 5

Example 5:

Equation 1: 4X − Y = 20

Equation 2: X + 4Y = 30

Find X and Y.

Answer: X = 6.47, Y = 5.88

Elimination Method

Since both equations do not have an equal coefficient, multiply equation (2) by 2.

Equation 1: 2X − Y = 20

Equation 2: X + 2Y = 30

2 × X + 2 × 2Y = 2 × 30

2X + 4Y = 60

Now, take away equation 2 from equation 1.

2X − Y = 20

2X + 4Y = 60

That is:

(-Y) – (+4Y) = 20 - 60

- 5Y = -40

Divide both sides by -5.

-5Y/-5 = -40/-5

Y = 8

Put this value in equation 1.

2X – Y = 20

That is:

2X – 8 = 20

Isolate 2X by adding 8 to both sides.

2X – 8 + 8 = 20 + 8

2X = 28

Divide both sides by 2.

2X/2 = 28/2

X = 14

Therefore, X= 14 and Y = 8.

Measures of Central Tendency

The measure of a central tendency is the average figure or value within a series of figures. There are three measures of central tendency. Let's take a look at each of them.

Arithmetic Mean

This is the average of a series of values. It is easily obtained by adding up all the figures and dividing the result by the total number of figures.

Example 1:

Calculate the average mean if 5 students in a class got these test scores: 40, 30, 45, 50 and 35.

Answer:

First, add up the figures.

40 + 30 + 45 + 50 + 35 = 200

Now, divide 200 by the total number of figures, which is 5.

Therefore, the arithmetic mean is 200/5 = 40

Example 2:

Farmers loaded up a truck with the following quantity of rice for each farmer: 50 kg, 80 kg, 60 kg, 10 kg, 40 kg, 20 kg, 70 kg, 30 kg. Calculate the average mean.

Answer:

First, add up the figures.

50 + 80 + 60 + 10 + 40 + 20 + 70 + 30 = 360

Now, divide 360 by the total number of figures, which is 8.

Therefore, the arithmetic mean is: 360/8 = 45

Median

The median is the mid-value when the figures are written in the order of magnitude.

Example 1:

What is the median of the following test scores? 40, 30, 45, 50, 35

Answer:

Rearrange the numbers to follow this sequence:

30, 35, 40, 45, 50

Now, count from the left and right. You will see that the median or middle value is 40.

The formula to solve for the median is:

n + 1 / 2, where n is the number of figures.

From the example above, n = 5.

Therefore, 5 + 1 / 2 = 6/2

= 3

The third figure after ordering is the median. This makes 40 the median.

Example 2:

What is the median of the following test scores? 40, 30, 45, 50, 35, 25

Answer:

The difference between this and the earlier example is the addition of one more number, which is 25, and this will affect the whole calculation.

Rearrange the numbers to follow this sequence:

25, 30, 35, 40, 45, 50

Now, count from the left and right. You will see that there are two numbers in the middle, 35 and 40. What should you do? Add both and divide by 2.

35 + 40/2 = 37.5

The median score is 37.5.

Use the formula n + 1/2 to solve for the median:

From the example above, n = 6.

Therefore, 6 + 1/2 = 7/2

= 3.5

None of the figures is 3.5. Therefore, add and divide the third and fourth terms by 2.

35 + 40/2 = 37.5

The median score is 37.5.

Mode

The mode is the most commonly occurring figure in a series of numbers.

Example 1:

What is the mode of this sequence? 3, 1, 2, 1, 5, 6, 3, 4, 1, 2

Answer:

To easily identify the mode, rearrange the numbers in order of magnitude.

1, 1, 1, 2, 2, 3, 3, 4, 5, 6

The mode (most commonly occurring number) is 1.

Example 2:

What is the mode of the following shoe sizes? 30, 40, 42, 38, 40, 38, 30, 41, 40, 35, 44

Answer:

Rearrange the numbers by order of magnitude.

30, 30, 35, 38, 38, 40, 40, 40, 41, 42, 44

The mode (the most commonly occurring shoe size) is 40.

Chapter 8: Economics

In Chapter 3, we broadly discussed the principles of the United States in international economics. This chapter discusses basic economic terms and concepts. These concepts include production, business organizations, supply and demand, economic systems and international trade.

Production

In economics, production is the creation of utility or goods and services and the satisfaction of desires or wants, which are remunerated in the form of payment. It is the utility of specific factors, which are also known as factors of production, for the creation of these goods and services.

Factors of Production

Production cannot be possible without the assembling and exploitation of the factors of production, which are land, labor, capital and enterprise.

Land

Land, in economics, is a natural resource that includes the earth's surface, the atmosphere (including the internet space), the water bodies and anything below the earth's surface. Land is a free gift of nature, and it is physically immobile.

Labor

This refers to all kinds of effort exerted toward the utility of available resources for production. Labor can be mental, manual, skilled or unskilled. Labor is often rewarded after the completion of a task.

Some economists prefer to call labor the prime mover because it is the initiator of all productive plans. Without labor, all other processes of production will become fallow.

Capital

This is an asset that is set aside to facilitate the production process. There are two broad classifications of capital.

1. Fixed capital: This includes fixed assets, such as buildings, implements, vehicles, etc.
2. Circulating capital: This is also called working capital, which is used to initiate production. It includes cash in hand, loans, overdrafts, shares and plowed-back profits. Circulating capital is, at times, called money capital.

Enterprise or entrepreneurship

Entrepreneurs are in charge of controlling and organizing all the factors of production for the purpose of production. They may be the directors, managers or owners of a public or private enterprise. They bear the risks involved in the production and distribution of goods and services.

The Law of Diminishing Returns

This law states that if there is an increase in the utility of a factor of production (like labor) while other factors (like land) remain constant, then there will, first of all, be an increase in return of production, followed by a fall. It is sometimes regarded as the law of variable proportion or non-proportional returns.

Business Organizations

Business organizations are entities or enterprises that are established by individuals, groups and the government. Let's examine the kinds of business organizations in a country.

Private enterprise

These are businesses that individuals or groups of individuals own and control. Except for nonprofit organizations, their primary goal is to make a profit. Ownership of a private enterprise can be in the form of a sole proprietorship, partnership, private limited liability company or cooperative.

Public enterprise

These are businesses that the government manages or controls. It can be urban councils or local, state or federal government. Public enterprises are for the interest of the community. They are targeted for equitable income distribution, employment and social security.

Sole proprietorship

This is a business that is managed and profitable to just one person. The person may receive assistance from family members. A sole proprietorship business is often very easy to organize, and the owner can make decisions without the obstacles of bureaucratic processes. A sole proprietorship business does not have limited liability. This means that creditors can seize the private assets of the sole proprietors if they fail to pay their debts.

Partnership

This is a business that consists of the resources of two to 20 individuals in the establishment and operations. Each partner has a quota of profits allotted based on agreement. Due to available collateral, the organization may take loans from banks.

Joint-stock company

This has a wider scope of ownership than a sole proprietorship or partnership. A lot of people can buy the organization's shares as a form of investment. Because of their capital size and rate of productivity, joint-stock companies have a great impact on the economy of the United States.

Investors or shareholders in joint-stock companies enjoy the advantage of limited liability and continuity, which these companies offer. They can either be private or public limited liability companies.

Private limited company

This consists of two to 50 owners who have bought shares in the company. The shares are not open for sale to the public, and a shareholder cannot sell a share without the consent of other shareholders. It also offers the advantage of limited liability. When there is a need for the liquidation of the company, it does not affect the shareholders' personal assets. Also, the company is a legal entity that can sue and be sued. It is subject to corporate tax.

Public limited company

These companies have a minimum of seven members. Shares are open for sales and acquisition to the public via the stock exchange market. Such companies can be financed through loans or the sales of shares. They offer limited liability to the shareholders.

Supply and Demand

These are complementary terms that play a salient role in every economy of the world. They affect the prices of goods and services in the market, and they determine the wealth of individuals, organizations and nations.

Demand

In economics, demand is the number of goods and services consumers are willing and have the capacity to buy at a defined price and time.

Demand is not always static. It is influenced by factors such as the price of the goods and services, the price of complementary and competing goods and services, income, population size, changes in preferences of consumers, environmental and social conditions and government policies.

Types of Demand

There are five general classifications of demand.

Competitive demand

Some goods and services have close substitutes. This means that there are other competitors who have similar goods and services. An example is the cell phone industry. When the price of any of these commodities increases, then more people may purchase the substitute and therefore there is an increase in the quantity of the substitute.

Derived demand

Some goods and services are required because of the demand for other products. For example, sugar and flour are needed for baked goods. Therefore, sugar and flour are examples of derived demand. Because people want good roads, there is a demand for skilled laborers. Skilled laborers, in this instance, are examples of derived demand.

Complementary or joint demand

When two items are both needed before they can give consumers maximal satisfaction, then both items are complementarily demanded. Examples are bread and butter or cereal and milk.

Composite demand

Some goods have different uses. An example is sugar, which can be used domestically and in industry. When there is a higher demand for industrial sugar, it will also affect the quantity of sugar produced for domestic use.

Independent demand

This applies to commodities that are not related in any way and are therefore not competing for the demand of consumers. For example, the demand for books is independent of the demand for clothes. Some economists, however, argue that no demand is ever independent because every commodity is contending for the purchasing power of household income.

Supply

Supply is the number of goods and services producers are willing to create and make available for consumption at a defined price and given period of time.

Supply is also not always stable. It is affected by factors like the price of the goods and services, the price of complementary and competing goods and services, income, population size, changes in preferences of consumers, environmental and social conditions and government policies.

Types of Supply

There are two types of supply.

Complementary or joint supply

Some commodities do not exist alone in production. They are produced with other commodities. One may be the by-product of another. An increase in the price of commodity A will lead to an increase in the price of commodity B. Examples are gasoline and kerosene, which are obtained from petroleum. Without petroleum, kerosene will not exist. An increase in the supply of one will lead to an increase in the supply of the other.

Composite supply

Products that are in composite supply are competitive in the market space. For example, different brands of cars, airplanes and motorcycles are all substitute means of transportation. A decrease in the price of one will lead to a decrease in the price of the other.

The Seven Laws of Supply and Demand

Here are the seven laws of demand and supply:

1. First law: There will be an increase in the quantity of goods or services demanded if there is a decrease in price.

2. Second law: There will be an increase in the quantity of goods or services supplied if there is an increase in price. When the price falls, there will be a decrease in supply too.

3. Third law: The process of adjustments is the place where supply and demand are at equilibrium.

4. Fourth law: The prices of goods and services fall when there is an increase in supply, and this will lead to an increase in demand.

5. Fifth law: When the supply of commodities decreases, the market price increases, and the demand reduces.

6. Sixth law: When the demand for commodities decreases, the market price reduces, and there is a contraction of supply.

7. Seventh law: When the demand for commodities increases, the market price increases, and there is an expansivity of supply.

Economic Systems in the World

Different economic systems exist all over the world. Here are some of the economic systems:

Capitalism

Capitalism requires private control of properties in the nation. In a capitalist state, there is a free enterprise that is regulated by governmental agencies. Private owners have the freedom to explore opportunities within the capacity of their capital. A capitalist state is highly competitive, and the primary pursuit is to make a profit. The United States is a capitalist society.

Socialism

In a socialist system, the means of production (that is, capital equipment and lands) are owned by the state. The primary goal is to invest in totality in society and not just in individuals. Unlike capitalism, there is collective ownership and control of large-scale production by the state or labor unions.

Socialism is based on equal distribution of wealth and resources in the state. It advocates for the social welfare of individuals in society.

Communism

Communism is the culmination of socialism. It is idealistic in principle. Just like socialism, all the means of production are completely owned by the community, which takes part in the income and the labor involved.

Communism is theoretically a process that goes through four stages of social evolution (bourgeois capitalism, then the dictatorship of the proletariat, which metamorphosizes into socialism and then culminates in communism). It tries to establish a classless society where everyone is rewarded according to their needs and abilities. It advocates for a system without wages, money or free exchange.

Examples of communist countries are Hungary, Yugoslavia, Russia and China.

Mixed Economic System

Individuals, who are also known as capitalists, and the government influence decisions regarding the management and control of production processes on a small and large scale. A mixed economy has qualities of both capitalism and socialism. It is argued that socialist/communist states, such as Hungary, Yugoslavia, Russia and China, still practice mixed economic systems.

International Trade

All foreign diplomats need to understand the basics of international trade. It is through international trade that countries exchange value and resources for stipulated amounts.

Why Do Nations Engage in Foreign Trade?

Nations trade for many reasons, including:

1. Geographical factors and different natural resources of nations.

2. Increase in population, which results in scarcity of available resources and need for the importation of more. For example, the United States has limited petroleum, so it still imports from other countries to make up for its lack.

3. Some countries have greater advantages and specialization in the production of resources, such as financial resources, human resources, land and mineral resources.

Barriers to International Trade

As much as international trade is needed, there are barriers that may hinder the fluidity of trade.

Currency – The differences in the value of currencies necessitate conversion in the foreign exchange market, and this limits the flow of goods.

Distance – The distance between countries and transportation systems affects international trade.

Tariffs – Although they are necessary for controlling import and export and are used to raise revenue, they are artificial barriers to international trade.

Language – The differences in language pose a barrier to effective communication.

Ideological differences – These can be political, economic or sociocultural.

Part B: Situational Judgment

Chapter 9: Procedures and Methods of Administration in the Foreign Service

In this chapter, we will be looking at the 14 principles of management of Henri Fayol and how they apply to the administration of the Foreign Service. Henri Fayol (1841–1925) was an executive who formulated a theory of business administration. These principles are relevant to all Foreign Service officers who will be managing human resources and other variables involved in the job.

The 14 principles are highlighted below.

1. Division of Labor

Fayol believed that when work is divided into units, then there will be greater productivity and quality of output. When there is an appropriate division of work, there is efficiency, speed and order. The number one rule in management is delegation. Tasks should be delegated to the best hands.

As a Foreign Service officer, you should be ready to divide tasks among team members. Collaboration is the easiest, fastest and most productive way of dealing with challenges. Apply the rule of specialization so that everyone gets to do what they are passionate about and skilled at.

Let's say there is a task to draft a 50-page document for your department and a deadline is given. The best way to approach this task is to identify those who are skilled in this area and divide the task into roles. There should be an assigned writer and at least two editors. Then the work can be delivered after editing.

2. Authority and Duties

If there must be quality management, then a recognized authority must be in place. The authority must understand his or her responsibilities and execute them without reservations. Everyone must know what their roles are in the department.

As a Foreign Service officer, you must always know who you directly report to and be sure there is no ambiguity in given instructions. There should be room for questioning for the purpose of clarity and redress on complex issues. Bureaucracy should not create communication or association gaps between the authorities/managing body and the employees.

3. Discipline

Discipline is an essential commodity for management. When there is no discipline, there will be no productivity. Discipline ensures that everyone does their job without unnecessary coercing or overbearing supervision. You must possess this quality if you plan to excel in the Foreign Service. Be disciplined about meeting deadlines, starting work early and delivering excellent results.

4. Unity of Command

Every employee or Foreign Service officer should report to just one boss. Multiple instructions from different bosses often result in confusion and conflict. This is called disunity in command.

Therefore, authorities should not interfere with the affairs of employees who are not directly below them. All decisions must be in alignment with the Constitution. It is lawful to disobey an order from your supervisor if the command is not consistent with the US Constitution.

5. Unity of Direction

Everyone in your department should be pursuing the same or similar goals. These goals must be specific, measurable, attainable, relevant to making an impact in the US economy and time-bound. That is why you should be aware of the decade, yearly, quarterly, monthly, weekly and daily goals of the current US administration and your department.

6. Subjugation of Personal Interests

Foreign Service officers are referred to as civil servants because they are in the field to serve the United States. It is wrong and unconstitutional to put your personal interests above your nation. Even if the situation conflicts with benefiting the nation of your origins, you must forgo personal sentiments and work toward US goals.

The command given may not be pleasing to you—maybe due to religion, personal idiosyncrasies, political stance or ethnic background—but you should comply with the order.

7. Reward

This is another factor that should be considered in management. A reward can be either financial or non-financial. It can be praise, recognition, a day off or something else. When leading a team, never expect that your employees' passion for service is all they need to get the task done. Remuneration is a source of motivation in every organization, and this includes the Foreign Service.

Remuneration should not be based on sentiments. It should be based on merit.

8. Centralization

Henri Fayol highlighted that the central body, or management, should maintain a neutral stance. He identified that a balanced approach to power-sharing is the best way to manage an organization. Power should not be top full and bottom empty, nor should it be the reverse.

9. Scalar Chain

Fayol stipulated that there is a need for a hierarchy, and this should start from the top and flow to the bottom. Every officer should have direct access to his or her superiors. This chain is needed for the transfer of information, promotion of officers and specialization in roles. As a Foreign Service officer, you should know who is above you and work with them.

10. Orderliness

When there is no orderliness, the new order will be frustration, lack of productivity and chaos. Seats, tables, decor and every aspect of the work environment should boost officer morale. Also, Foreign Service officers must be psychologically and physically sound because these aspects affect a person's quality of work.

11. Equity and Fairness

In the workplace, you should treat everyone with equity. There should be no racial, gender, religious, or personal biases. No employee or customer should face discrimination. For example, it is common for some people to categorize all Muslims as terrorists and therefore treat individuals from this background with suspicions and prejudice.

Some people still practice White supremacy. They believe people with White skin color are superior to people from other races, and they transfer this misconception to the workplace.

12. Job Security

A worker tends to work better if there is stability in the workplace. If the administration offers job security, fewer penalties and an enabling environment, employees will feel safe investing their time and effort.

13. Initiative

Authorities should encourage initiative. When workers see that their initiatives are recognized, they will do more. No matter how insignificant the initiative may seem, employees should be listened to and taken seriously.

Initiative is the hallmark of exceptional Foreign Services officers. As a Foreign Service officer, you have to take an innovative approach toward problem-solving. Do not be too traditional or conservative in your methodologies. Be open to new ideas. Stay process minded, but more importantly, be results oriented.

14. Esprit de Corps

In the work arena, there should be trust, understanding and loyalty to the mission. Foreign Service officers must always put their nation first. To be productive, you will have to communicate and liaise with other Foreign Service officers who share the same values as you.

Chapter 10: Principles of Management, Human Behavior and Psychology

The job of a Foreign Service officer demands an understanding of human psychology and behavior. You should be able to manage situations wisely. Therefore, in the FSOT, you will be asked questions that test the depth of your knowledge of situations requiring astute judgment.

The Principles of Psychology and Human Management

In layman's terms, psychology is the study and prediction of human behavior and actions. Since the job of a Foreign Service officer demands interaction and mingling with humans, you need to know how humans behave and why they take certain actions.

Psychology

Interpersonal relationships play a major role in the workplace. Understanding the psychology of the workplace helps reduce the complexities, misunderstandings and stress associated with working with people.

Psychologists have categorized psychology into the study of the environment or office and the nature of people who work there. This is termed organizational and workplace psychology.

Workplace psychology is meant to improve the working conditions in the work environment. It is meant to identify and eliminate issues or complications in the workplace, make employees feel at ease, serve customers optimally and facilitate effectiveness.

The organizational aspect of workplace psychology focuses on team building through training and efficiency in productivity.

Before you become a Foreign Service officer, you need to be acquainted with the Team, Emotional and Social Intelligence (TESI) Model of workplace psychology. It highlights seven skills that are needed for building an effective team and work experience. These skills are:

1. Team Identity

When team members understand themselves, it will be easier to get tasks done. Workers must understand the vision and mission and be technically fit for the task.

When we say team members must understand themselves, we are simply referring to basic elements like temperaments, strengths, weaknesses, motivations and perspectives.

2. Motivation

As earlier highlighted in the principles of management, motivation is a key factor in the workplace. Foreign Service officers who are motivated through monetary or other forms of reward tend to be more productive. Humans are wired to stake their time and efforts on things that will gratify them personally.

Apply this rule when dealing with people as a diplomat. Do not be too quick to make your interests obvious. Allow the second party to see how they will benefit from a deal or negotiation, and everyone goes home a winner.

Diplomats must be astute in motivating parties to make favorable decisions that are beneficial to the United States.

3. Emotional Awareness

To have a successful career in the Foreign Service, you must learn the art of emotional awareness. For effective collaboration, you must take the other person's emotional state into consideration. Humans like to give their time, attention and approval to people who seem to understand them or what they do.

4. Communication

Much of your function as a Foreign Service officer will require communication. In the field, you must know how to communicate with clients and other personnel. In Chapter 12, we discuss how you can effectively communicate with your audience.

5. Stress Tolerance

Too much work will lead to a lack of productivity. Do not stress yourself or others.

6. Conflict Resolution

Where there are humans, conflicts should be expected. Therefore, it is important you see crises in the workplace as situations that cannot be totally avoided. Be diplomatic, impartial and equitable when resolving conflicts. Listen to all sides before passing judgment.

7. Positive Mood

Keep your mood positive and upbeat when relating with people. A positive mood will bring out the best in those around you. Instead of being tense or antagonistic, being positive yourself will make others feel relaxed and ready to work for the good of the organization.

Managing People with Different Temperaments

As you go about your job as a Foreign Service officer, be ready to work with people of different temperaments. When you master the four temperament types, you will be able to work well with people, judiciously react to situations and manage affairs productively.

Temperament

Temperament is the behavior of people based on their inherent traits and experiences in the world.

There are four kinds of temperaments: sanguine, choleric, phlegmatic and melancholic. Most people have a combination of two or more of these temperaments, yet one is dominant while the others are secondary. The dominant temperament is called the primary temperament, while the recessive temperament is secondary.

1. Sanguine

Sanguine is a temperament of extroversion. People in this category like to go out. They derive joy from relating with people. They relish teamwork and engaging in fellowship.

Their enthusiasm is contagious. This quality is what makes you feel relaxed when you are with them. Sanguines do not know how to hide their feelings, and that is why people tend to trust them in relationships.

Sanguines have a carefree, affectionate nature. They love acceptance and loathe rejection. Another wonderful trait about sanguines is that they are playful and very optimistic.

When dealing with sanguines, learn to be patient with them. Allow them to do most of the talking and listen attentively to what they are saying. They are more likely to follow you if you show that you understand their perceptions. However, be careful about how much confidential information you disclose to them because they are likely to share information with others.

2. Choleric

Cholerics are goal-driven individuals who set goals and do all they can to achieve those goals. They have a positive attitude toward their plans and are not discouraged even when they face obstacles.

When you see someone who is very practical about life and more focused on getting desired results, then you have met a choleric. Cholerics can be overconfident of their opinions, independent, rude and extroverted.

Cholerics are very assertive with their decisions. They are quick in carrying out their plans, and they take risks. Cholerics like to be in charge. Therefore, they do not mind making decisions for others, and this attitude makes them seem domineering.

Cholerics are often consumed with tasks to complete. They will never bow to peer pressure, but they tend to pressure others to do their biddings. Cholerics do not make friends easily. Instead, they prefer to be independent and have a very small circle of friends.

When you hear cholerics talking, you will think they are angry, but you may be mistaken. Their tempers or demeanors frequently burn hot when they fail to get an important task done. Do not expect empathy from cholerics. Their undivided passion is often for goals or causes.

If you have a choleric as a team member, your goal should be to make them see the reasons and importance of the goal. Then they will be ready to put forth ideas and efforts to see the team succeed.

3. Phlegmatic

Phlegmatics are often passive about life issues, even regarding things others consider to be very important. They prefer to stick to what they are used to. You know that a colleague is phlegmatic if the person is calm, easygoing, ambivalent and ready to take instructions from others.

Nonetheless, when carrying out your diplomatic duty, do not expect someone with a phlegmatic temperament to easily accommodate you or anyone else. You will usually find phlegmatics in conservative or quiet areas. Learn to respect their quiet moments. Give them time to cogitate on matters when there is an issue that requires a decision.

A phlegmatic's loyalty is not to be questioned, but they find it difficult to resume broken relationships. Therefore, do your best to earn their trust, but do not disappoint them after they have given you their loyalty and commitment.

4. Melancholy

Melancholics are often very cautious when making decisions. They are often obsessed with details and are most times seen as perfectionists. They tend to operate by the book.

Melancholics are introverted, analytical, logical and great planners. They often regret past mistakes and worry about what the future holds. They are suspicious about almost everyone, and they love to please their conscience.

When working with melancholics, be ready to give details of plans or activities. They expect you to be very knowledgeable about whatever you are telling them.

Do not be in a hurry to get them to decide, because they will not do so until they have done their homework and are certain of their plans. Do not get annoyed when they pick out inconspicuous mistakes that are normally overlooked.

Part C: English Expressions

Chapter 11: English Usage

English has become a global language. It is spoken in every continent of the world even though it is not an official language in some countries.

As a Foreign Service diplomat, you will be speaking to people across various territories of the world. You need to have a thorough understanding of the usage of English.

Parts of Speech

The parts of speech are groups into which words or lexical items are classified. In English, there are basically eight parts of speech: noun, verb, adjective, adverb, pronoun, conjunction, preposition and interjection. For practicality and FSOT purpose, we will delve more deeply into nouns and verbs.

Nouns

A noun is a naming word. It is the name of a person, animal, place, idea, subject, or anything you can think of. Examples are:

• Person: Samuel, John, Bob, etc.

• Animal: Lassie, Sassy, cat, dog, etc.

• Place: Washington, DC, France, Asia, Chicago, etc.

• Idea: Love, joy, peace, comfort, etc.

• Subject: English, mathematics, economics, chemistry, etc.

Types of Nouns

There are seven types of nouns: proper nouns, common nouns, concrete nouns, abstract nouns, countable nouns, uncountable nouns (or mass nouns) and collective nouns.

Proper Nouns

Nouns of specific identities are capitalized. They can be:

• Specific persons: James, Juliet, Benedict, Gladys

• Specific places: Chicago, Taiwan, Africa, Switzerland

• Specific days: Monday, Tuesday, Wednesday, Thursday

• Specific months: January, February, March

• Specific newspapers and magazines: *New York Times, Forbes, The Guardian*

As seen above, proper nouns do not normally take plural forms, and they are not often preceded by articles. However, there are exceptions to this rule.

• A proper noun may take an indefinite article, *a* or *an*, if it is referring to the quality of someone in the past and not the current personality. Examples are:

1. A Roosevelt is here. (This could be referring to a family member.)

2. I have just seen a Lincoln. (This could be referring to a work of art.)

• A proper noun may also take the definite article *the* when it is specifically in reference to someone. Examples are:

1. The Shakespeare of our time has written a new poem.

2. He is the Adolf Hitler of Europe.

Common Nouns

These nouns are not specific to a particular entity. They are general names shared by entities of that nature. Examples are:

• Persons: boy, girl, sister, man, etc.

• Animals: cat, dog, fish, goat, etc.

• Places: village, city, nation, school, etc.

• Things: biscuit, cake, juice, etc.

• Ideas: hatred, love, peace, etc.

Concrete Nouns

These are nouns that we can see and touch. They include most common and proper nouns. Examples are *boy*, *girl*, *mountain*, *oranges*, *Peter*, etc.

Abstract Nouns

These are nouns that we cannot see and touch. We can, however, feel or perceive them. They include common and proper nouns. Examples are *harmony*, *goodness*, *faithfulness*, etc.

Countable Nouns

These are nouns that are often categorized by their individualities. These nouns take plural forms and can be preceded by articles *a*, *an* and *the*.

The plural of countable nouns can be formed in different ways, such as:

- Adding -*s* to the base of the noun. i.e., boy/boys, rat/rats
- Adding -*es* to the base of the noun. i.e., church/churches
- Mutation, which is the changing of the base word. i.e., tooth/teeth, mouse/mice, louse/lice
- Adding -*en* to the base word. i.e., child/children, ox/oxen
- Using a native or foreign form. i.e., syllabus - syllabuses – syllabi
- Not adding any suffix. This is known as zero plural. i.e., sheep/sheep

Note that there are words that are naturally plurals. They are called summation plurals because they consist of two parts that are equal in size. Examples are *glasses, binoculars, pajamas, scissors, pliers, trousers, spectacles, pants*, etc.

These should not be used with singular verbs unless they are attached with *a pair of* or other kinds of partitives.

• The glasses are mine. ✓

• The glasses is mine. X

• The glass is mine. X

However, if you want to identify the entities by their units, you can say:

• I have a pair of glasses. ✓

• Take two pairs of glasses. ✓

Mass Nouns

These are nouns that are seen as not having a natural bond. They are also known as uncountable nouns or non-count nouns. Examples are *water, furniture, equipment, grass, land, bread, information, blood, advice, chalk, luggage, sugar, ice, business, news, milk, beer*, etc.

They are gradable or quantifiable through specific expressions, such as a stick of chalk, a blade of grass, an item of business, etc.

Verbs

Verbs are action words. They tell us about a state of being and can be used to show possibilities, ability and obligation. Examples are:

• Action words: *go, come, play, shout, sing, look, etc.*

• State of being: *is, was, am, being, be, were, are*

• Possibility: *may, might*

• Ability: *can, could*

• Obligation: *should, shall, ought to*

The Forms of Verbs

Verbs often have five forms. They are:

1. The base form: It does not take any inflection. It is also the plural form of verbs. It should be used with plural nouns or subjects. Examples are *say, sing, fight, dance, report, open.*

2. The -*s* form: This is the singular form of the verb. It should be used with singular nouns or subjects. It is often inflected with an -*s*. Examples are *says, sings, fights, dances, reports, opens.*

3. The -*ed 1* form: This is the past tense form of verbs. It tells us that an action has been taken in the past. It often takes a suffix of -*ed* if the verb is a regular verb. If it is an irregular verb, it will change its form. Examples are *said, danced, reported, opened, sang, fought.*

4. The -*ed 2* form: This is the perfective aspect of verbs. It tells us that an action has been completed in the present or in the past. It often takes a suffix of -*ed* if the verb is a regular verb. If it is an irregular verb, it will change its form. These verbs are often used with a preceding *has, had,* or *had* (except in passive voice). Examples are *said, danced, seen, broken, stolen, sung, rung.*

Always remember that:

• *Has* is used with a singular subject.

• *Have* is used with a plural subject.

• *Had* is the past tense of *has* and *have.*

5. The -*ing* form: This is the progressive form of a verb. It can be in the present (by adding a preceding present tense) or in the past (by adding a preceding past tense). Examples are *saying, dancing, breaking, singing, reporting.*

Adjectives

An adjective is a descriptive word that describes a noun or a pronoun. Examples are *ugly, beautiful, fat, short, wise, tall,* etc. Adjectives often precede nouns and can be compared in the comparative *(-er, more)* and superlative forms *(-est, most)*. Examples include:

• I have a big house.

• Look at the wise man.

• The girl is taller than her classmates.

Adverbs

An adverb modifies the action of a verb, the description of an adjective or another adverb. Adverbs often end in *-ly*, *-wise*, or *-ward*. Examples are *slowly, happily, angrily, clockwise, backward*. Other examples of adverbs that do not take inflections are *however, furthermore, very, only, since*, among others.

Examples:

• Why are you dancing so <u>happily</u>?

• He looked <u>angrily</u> at the man.

• The king is <u>very</u> handsome.

Pronouns

Pronouns are used in place of nouns. They are used to avoid the repetition of nouns in a statement. A summary of pronouns is seen in this table:

Person	Case	Singular	Plural
1st person	Subjective	I	we
	Objective	me	us
	Possessive	my, mine	our, ours
2nd person	Subjective	you	you
	Objective	you	you
	Possessive	your	yours
3rd person	Subjective	Masculine: he	they
		Feminine: she	they
		Neuter: it	they
	Objective	Masculine: him	them
		Feminine: her	them
		Neuter: it	them
	Possessive	Masculine: his	
		Feminine: her	their, theirs
		Neuter: its	

Pronouns should be used according to their classifications:

The Subjective: This includes *he, she, it, I, we, you* and *they*. These pronouns should come before the main verb except for questions. Illustrative examples are:

• <u>He</u> arrived on Wednesday.

• <u>She</u> likes to dance.

The Objective: This includes *him, her, it, me, us, you* and *them*. These pronouns should come after the main verb. Illustrative examples are:

• They called <u>him</u> on Wednesday.

• I have given <u>her</u> the book.

The Possessive: This includes *his, her, hers, its, my, mine, their, theirs, your, yours, our* and *ours*. These pronouns are used to show ownership. Illustrative examples are:

• <u>Your</u> (not *yours*) book is on the table.

• The book is <u>yours </u>(not *your*).

• <u>My</u> (not *mine*) car is in the park.

• The car is <u>mine</u> (not *my*).

Conjunctions

Conjunctions are used to combine phrases and clauses, show contrast or suggest an alternative. Examples are *and, or, but, also*, etc. Illustrative examples are:

• John <u>and</u> Betty are getting married.

• You came to visit <u>but</u> left early.

• Should I go <u>or</u> should I stay?

Prepositions

Prepositions connect or link other grammatical items together. Examples are *to, in, on, with, across*. Illustrative examples are:

• He is sitting <u>on</u> the chair.

• I came to the office <u>with</u> a heavy heart.

• The man is <u>in</u> his house.

Interjections

Interjections are used when there is an exclamation to make. They are identified with an exclamation point (!). They are often used to show surprise, pain, anger or joy. Illustrative examples are:

• Oh no! I have missed my flight.

• Wow! We did it!

Articles

There are generally three articles in the English language. They are *a, an* and *the*.

• *A* and *an* are indefinite articles. They are used mostly when we are not sure of the identification. Article *a* precedes words that begin with consonant sounds, while article *an* precedes words that begin with vowel sounds. Illustrative examples are:

• <u>A</u> boy came here and sat down.

• I saw <u>a</u> strange man yesterday.

• *The* is a definite article. It is used when we are sure of the identified entity. Illustrative examples are:

• <u>The</u> man is hungry.

• <u>The</u> girl is tired.

Concord

Concord is the agreement between grammatical items. In the English language, there are certain rules guiding the arrangement and choice of grammatical items when constructing sentences.

Rule 1: Use singular subjects with singular verbs.

You will know a verb is singular when you see *-s* attached to it.

• He <u>likes</u> me.

• My teacher <u>comes</u> to school on time.

Rule 2: Use plural subjects with plural verbs.

You will know a verb is plural when there is no inflection on it.

• They <u>like</u> me.

• My teachers <u>come</u> to school on time.

Invariables

A. There are some singular nouns that look like plurals because they take the *-s* form, but they are not plural. These should be used with singular verbs. Examples are *mathematics, linguistics, gymnastics, athletics, measles, Athens, Algiers, news, barracks,* etc.

• Linguistics <u>is</u> a simple course.

• Measles <u>was</u> once prevalent in some states.

B. There are also some plural nouns that look like singular nouns because they do not take the *-s* form. They should always be used with plural verbs. Examples are *cattle, clergy, people.*

• The cattle <u>are</u> grazing.

- Why <u>are</u> the clergy worried about the issue?

- The people <u>were</u> very hungry.

Rule 3: Ignore words that look like the coordinator *and* though they are not.

These are called pseudo coordinators because they look like coordinators. But you should not assign the combinatory or pluralizing function of *and* to them unless the subject is plural.

This includes *as well as, in addition to, in the company of, alongside, in conjunction with*, etc. They should not affect the nature of the verb—that is, if the verb is singular or plural. Instead, focus on the subject. If the subject is singular and these pseudo coordinators are used, use a singular verb. Use a plural verb for plural subjects.

- <u>The Foreign Service officer,</u> as well as his children, <u>is</u> traveling tomorrow.

The subject in this statement is *the Foreign Service officer* and it is singular. Therefore, the verb should be singular.

- <u>The Congressmen,</u> in conjunction with the Senate, <u>are</u> having a meeting.

The subject in this statement is *the Congressmen* and it is plural. Therefore, the verb should be plural.

- <u>The director general,</u> with his wife, <u>is</u> celebrating his birthday.

The subject in this statement is *the director general* and it is singular. Therefore, the verb should be singular.

Rule 4: Use singular verbs for two units that portray a singular idea even though they are combined with *and*.

- <u>Rice and stew is</u> my favorite food.

- <u>Chicken and rice was</u> served at the party.

Rule 5: Use singular verbs for phrases and clauses that are titles, names, or quotations even if they seem like plural words.

- *Romeo and Juliet* <u>is</u> a good play.

- "<u>To be or not to be</u>" <u>is</u> a line in a Shakespearean play.

- <u>Shooting unarmed civilians</u> <u>is</u> unlawful.

Rule 6: Whenever a relative pronoun (*that, whom, which, who*) is used, the verb should agree with the phrase that precedes it.

- <u>The diplomat</u> <u>whom</u> we have been waiting for <u>is</u> here.

- <u>The girl</u> <u>who</u> was crying <u>was</u> helped.

- This is <u>the soldier</u> who <u>was</u> on duty.

Rule 7: Fractions or percentages often take either singular or plural verbs. What should be considered is the item that comes with the *of* phrase.

- <u>One-third</u> of the <u>building</u> <u>has</u> been destroyed.

- <u>Three-quarters</u> of the police <u>officers</u> <u>were</u> in the meeting.

- Seventy percent of <u>the presidents</u> have arrived.

Rule 8: When the lexical item *number of* is used, the verb should be singular if the statement starts with the definite article *the*. However, it should be plural if the statement starts with the indefinite articles *a* and *an*.

- <u>The</u> number of US officials <u>is</u> around fifty.

- <u>A</u> number of houses <u>have</u> been demolished.

- <u>A</u> number of parents <u>were</u> here.

Rule 9: If the noun is a unit of measurement and there is a premodifier that comes before it, the verb should be singular.

- Sixty pounds <u>is</u> too heavy for me to carry.

- Two miles <u>was</u> measured.

Rule 10: The rule of proximity states that the verb should take after the form of the subject that immediately comes after an *either* phrase or a *neither* phrase.

• Either the man or <u>his parents</u> <u>are</u> coming to the party.

• Either the public relations officer or <u>the farmer</u> <u>has</u> been in the consulate.

• Neither the writer nor <u>the editors</u> <u>like</u> to work.

Idiomatic Expressions

Idiomatic expression is an aspect of the English language that shows how diverse and rich the language is. While working as a diplomat, you will come across people who are very proficient in the usage of English, and it is essential you have knowledge of idiomatic expressions so that you will not "be at sea" in the conversation.

Examples of idioms include:

Stir up a hornet's nest: This means to cause trouble.

Example: Management is keeping silent about the issue because they don't want to stir up a hornet's nest.

Back against the wall: This means being in a hard situation without a way out.

Example: He has done all he can, and now it seems his back is against the wall.

Head over heels: If someone is head over heels, it means the person is totally in love.

Example: You have fallen for Jesse; you are head over heels.

Upset a person's applecart: It means to cause someone's plan to fail.

Example: The US government may soon have a ban on immigration. This will upset the applecart of prospective immigrants.

Up in arms: It means to not be happy about something.

Example: The basketball team is up in arms against the rival sports team that cheated in the championship.

Scrape the barrel: It means you have decided to fall back to something you did not intend to use because it is the only alternative you have.

Example: I had to scrape the barrel when I had to voluntarily drop out of school after my benefactor died.

Bend over backward: This means putting forth your best attitude to accommodate or please someone even if it is uncomfortable for you.

Example: The woman had to bend over backward to make her husband stop the divorce process.

Make no bones about it: This means stating clearly how you feel or your thoughts about something.

Example: Jim made no bones about it when he was asking for a salary increase.

Break new ground: This means doing what has never been achieved before.

Example: Scientists are breaking new ground every year.

In the same breath: This applies to making two statements that are contradictory.

Example: The instructor tells us he studied English and says he doesn't know about syntax in the same breath.

Burn the candle at both ends: This means to be too busy with work or any activity that consumes time and energy.

Example: Tom burned the candle at both ends when he was young. Now he is reaping the benefits.

Against the clock: This means being in a hurry in order to make up for lost time.

Example: When I discovered that there was so much work that needed to be done, I started working against the clock.

Chicken-and-egg situation: This is a situation in which it's hard to determine how one factor leads to another.

Example: My boss blames me for the failed presentation. I blame my boss for not giving me appropriate guidance. Either way, we didn't win the new account. It's a chicken-and-egg situation regarding who is really at fault.

On cloud nine: This means to be very happy.

Example: The girl was on cloud nine when she aced her exam.

Head in the clouds: It means to live in a dreamlike world.

Example: Why do you have your head in the clouds?

Small cog in a large wheel: It means when something or someone is a part of a bigger plan.

Example: I work as a cleaner at the university. I see myself as a small cog in a large wheel.

Left out in the cold: It means to be ignored.

Example: The boy was trying to get his teacher's attention, but he was left out in the cold.

Pour cold water on: It means to criticize a plan or idea.

Example: The congressmen poured cold water on the secretary's plans.

To come to a head: This means to reach a state of conflict or crisis.

Example: The issue came to a head when the army started killing innocent citizens.

Punctuation

Punctuation helps readers understand written text. It is used to ensure fluency while reading and prevent distortion of the message the writer is conveying.

Here are some punctuation marks and how they are used:

1. Full stop or period (.)

It shows where a sentence ends.

Example: My favorite color is green. It is the color of our environment.

A period is also used for abbreviations. Example: *Jr.* and *Dr.*

2. The Comma (,)

The comma ensures fluency in a text. It is the most used punctuation mark after the period. The comma is used to separate sentences or ideas that depend on each other. The period is used to separate expressions that are complete.

Example: The man is big, and the children are taller than him.

A comma should be used before the coordinating conjunction *and* to divide the two sentence clauses.

3. Quotation Marks (")

Quotation marks are used in direct speech or to emphasize a point.

Example: "When you are happy," he said, "you look more beautiful."

Example: The man is the "sun" of his home.

4. Parentheses ( )

Parentheses are used to add an extra piece of information.

Example: The market (which is very busy today) is on Elm Street.

5. Square Brackets [ ] and Ellipses (...)

These are used to show that new content has been added or deleted from the original text. Ellipses are also used to show that there is discontinuity from the main thought.

Example: The man [who resided in St. Petersburg] traveled to New York.

Example: When you think about it...it's not the world's worst idea.

6. Question Mark (?)

This is used after asking a question.

Example: Where are you?

7. Exclamation point (!)

This is used to express an unexpected outcry of joy, pain or surprise.

Example: "My gosh! How did you do it?"

8. Semicolon (;)

This is mostly used to connect two independent clauses. One of the sentences may be explaining the other.

Example: William was tired; he thought it was because of the pain in his leg.

9. Colon (:)

This is used to introduce items. It is also used to introduce the explanation of a preceding clause.

Example: The list stated, "Buy me the following: apples, pears and grapes."

10. Hyphen and Dash

One is often used for the other because they look so much alike. But the two are not the same.

A dash is often used to break words down into statements. It has two types: the em dash and the en dash.

Em dash (—): It is longer than the other type of dash, and it is used just like the semicolon or colon.

En dash (–): It is twice as long as the hyphen but shorter than an em dash. It is used to show range or connection.

Example: 1876–2013 (en dash)

Harry arrived on time—just as he always has. (em dash)

• Hyphen (-) combines compound words.

Examples: *part-time, well-being*

11. The Apostrophe (')

This shows that letters have been omitted in a word or abbreviation. Examples are *won't, I've, it's, 'cause.*

It is also used in the possessive case. Example: *This is Peter's pen.*

It is used to show the plural of lowercase letters. Example: *i's* and *t's.*

How to Write a Quality Essay

An essay is a piece of writing that intends to communicate a message, information, or opinion. Generally, all essays are written in three parts: introduction, body and conclusion.

• Introduction: This is often the first paragraph of your essay. This is where you present your position in an argument.

• Body: This is the second and subsequent paragraphs before the final paragraph. This is where you support your points in each paragraph.

• Conclusion: This is the final paragraph of your essay. It summarizes your argument and may end with a tone of finality.

When writing your essay, follow these guidelines:

1. Make a list of your best points.

2. Organize your points logically or coherently. One point should flow to another in your essay. Do not include irrelevant points.

3. Support your points in each paragraph. Show that you have knowledge of the point you are supporting. The tone of your writing should be persuasive.

4. Avoid grammatical blunders and spell words correctly. Make use of correct punctuation marks.

5. Edit your essay by going through it more than once.

Chapter 12: Effective Communication

Effective communication is not only for those who are in the field of communication. Everyone needs to know how to communicate effectively. As a Foreign Service officer, this is a skill you must practice until you master it. In your FSOT, you will be tested on English expressions. Effective communication makes up an aspect of this section.

Let's first take a look at the qualities of effective speakers before we discuss how to communicate effectively.

Qualities of Effective Speakers

Effective speaking is not straightforward. Effective speaking is more than just talking or sending your message to an audience.

To be a Foreign Service officer who communicates with people effectively, you have to understand and implement some essential communication tools. When you are speaking effectively, your audience wants to hear more. You will need to connect with your audience through storytelling, entertainment, word choice, the content of your speech and your style of communication. Here are five essential qualities you must possess if you want to become a Foreign Service officer who knows how to connect with people.

1. Confidence

Confidence is a very important quality when it comes to effective speaking. It makes people see you as an expert and therefore they tune into what you are saying. To show confidence, you must first believe in yourself and the message you are communicating.

2. Passion

Be passionate about the message you want someone else to buy into. Why should someone else believe what you are unsure of? If you are ambivalent about or disinterested in the information you are sharing with your audience, it will reflect in how energetically you communicate. People will believe almost anything as long as the speaker is sincerely passionate about the information.

Before you speak on foreign policy as a US delegate, you must have studied the policy, understand it and be totally convinced that it is right.

3. Conciseness

Effective speakers are concise. Audience members often do not have a long attention span, and their minds may wander if a speech digresses for too long.

Effective speakers know where to begin their presentation and when to stop. Divide your speech into segments and allow room for the audience to participate, contribute and ask questions. When your audience is involved in the communication process, they are less likely to give their attention to something else.

4. Storytelling Skills

Interesting stories keep an audience's attention. If you tell stories instead of just stating facts, your audience will give you their undivided attention. Stories help people retain information. They help your audience see the life application or practicality of the information.

5. Environmental Consciousness

Speaking goes beyond you and your message. It also includes the person or audience you are communicating with. Effective speakers always desire to understand the audience. They want to know their sociocultural background, political views, religious beliefs and other characteristics.

If you are sent to be an ambassador in a foreign nation, you should study about the people you will be relating with. Read up about other people's experiences there. Look for a friendly local who can give you a head's up on what you should expect.

How to Speak Effectively

Your daily life will be filled with communication when you begin a Foreign Service career. You will come across different people of different backgrounds. Therefore, you must learn to communicate in a manner that is understandable, purposeful and effective. So, how do you communicate effectively as a Foreign Service officer?

1. Ensure the Environment Is Ideal

Be conscious of the time, atmosphere and place setting where you are. An environment filled with noise and disorderliness will distort the flow of communication.

Understand that every conversation has its own suitable environment. If the discussion contains exclusive information that should not be known to the public, then find a private place to communicate.

The time of discussion also matters. Avoid discussing heavy matters in the evening or nighttime. Save these conversations for morning and afternoon, when everyone is fully alert.

Eliminate every source of distraction that may inhibit the flow of conversation. You can either turn off your phone or put it on silent. If you cannot control the noise or distractions around you, then find a more suitable environment.

2. Set up Communications

Effective communication involves planning what you are going to say in your mind, verbally or as written notes before the presentation. You may want to list the key points that will serve as a reminder when speaking. This approach will help you be succinct.

Highlight the purpose of the discussion. If it is a one-way speech, be direct with your points. Use repetition for emphasis.

3. Mind Your Speech

If you are giving a public speech to a group of people, you may want to begin with an anecdote. Anecdotes help to put the audience at ease because they are often what the audience can relate to.

Also, choose simple words instead of vague vocabulary. Everyone should understand your choice of words.

Remember to enunciate your words clearly. The volume of your voice should be audible for all to hear. Your tone should be steady. You may want to increase the pitch and repeat lines when addressing key points.

Avoid using a monotone in your communication. It is better to use a variety of tones. This is known as vocal color.

When you are switching from one point or topic to another, increase the pitch of your voice. Stay fluent when speaking, but pause whenever you are about to emphasize a key word.

Effective communication means being clear, understood and concise. Practice what you will say in front of the mirror or a friend.

4. Be Attentive

Communication is a two-way street that requires the speaker to listen to the audience. Ask for feedback. It will help you learn the needs, desires, backgrounds and motives of the people you are addressing.

Sometimes, the audience may seem to be paying attention, but they're actually not listening to you, or they may not understand what you are saying. To resolve this issue, engage the individual or group in contributing to what you have been saying.

5. Observe and Acknowledge the Audience's Feelings

People are not robots. They have feelings, which you must acknowledge if you want to be successful in communicating with them. Showing your audience that you understand how they are feeling will make them feel at ease and open up to you.

6. Use Body Language

Acknowledge people by looking in their direction or calling on them for greater participation when you see them nodding or displaying interest in what you are saying.

Be conscious of your body movements. Your facial expressions matter. Frowning or raising your brow may send a negative message to your audience. Every society has body languages that are considered taboo. You should try to learn some of these movements in order to avoid creating misunderstandings between you and your audience.

Watch out for expressions that show negativity. Some of these expressions cut across various cultures, and you may be familiar with them. Some of these negative, nonverbal communications include clenching the fist, frowning, slouching and silence.

Learn to build eye contact with your audience. It shows that you are confident and truthful. Two to four seconds is enough to establish eye contact with one person. Then move on to another person. Do this with everyone because if a person in the group sees that you are not giving them attention, they may detach or ignore what you are saying. That may cost you a business deal or an opportunity to make an impact.

However, in some cultures, eye contact is seen as offensive or unsettling. You will notice this by how your audience responds to you.

Hand gestures are also tools of communication. Observe the message your hands are conveying. You may use your hands when listing, pointing or demonstrating something. Some hand gestures are, however, distracting or inappropriate in certain cultural contexts. As a diplomat, you must be observant of these cultural differences so you know what is acceptable and what is not. Through the audience reaction or other speakers, you will know if you should continue such gestures or do away with them.

Remember: Your body is a tool for communication. Use it well.

7. Pause

When you pause, it gives the audience an opportunity to pay more attention to what is coming next. Pausing gives your listeners some time to think about and digest what you have said. It is a way of making your words more compelling.

Take a deep breath before continuing as this will help you stay steady while communicating. It gives you time to review your notes or the knowledge you have stored in your mind.

8. Check Yourself

Speaking is not just about the audience but also about you and the message. As you speak, assess your body movements. Are you shuffling, sneezing or sniffling? All of these will negatively affect the impact of your communication.

It is a good idea to record your discussions or presentations. Then play the recording later to assess performance. You will be able to identify unintended body language that you need to avoid in your next presentation or communication with other diplomats.

How to Effectively Communicate When Conflict Arises

Every diplomat should know how to handle conflict using the power of words, composure and sound judgment. Here is a step-by-step guide that will help you communicate effectively:

1. Be at the same level with the conflicting party/parties. Avoid taking sides. If they are sitting, take a seat. If they are standing, it is best to stand up with them. This action will prevent uneasiness or power struggles.

2. Listen to what they have to say. Do not be in a hurry to make assumptions and pass judgment based on what you see. Hasty judgments often end up being erroneous. Wait until the other parties have finished before you start talking.

3. Use a calm voice. If your voice is naturally loud, tone it down. Avoid getting angry or venting your anger on someone who seems to be at fault. Maintain a calm composure.

4. After someone has spoken, let them know you have heard all their points. You may have to restate the key points they have made so that they know you understood them perfectly.

5. You do not need to conclude the argument at that time. The other party may refuse to talk, or they may get angry and walk out. Do not go after them. Be patient and wait until they are calm.

6. Sometimes you will have to let things be. Do not try to win a verbal bout by getting the last word in. Sometimes you just have to be indifferent or agree to what the other speaker is saying as long as agreeing to disagree does not cost you anything. What matters is that everyone moves on.

7. Master the use of *I* when relaying your concerns. When someone does something you do not like, avoid blaming it all on the person. This will make them more empathetic and help them see reason with you.

For example, instead of saying, "You are lazy, and it makes me want to hit you," say, "I understand that we sometimes find it difficult to get things done the way we want to. This affects other important things we do. I feel you will achieve more if you increase your work ethic."

You will be surprised at how people begin to respond to your empathetic suggestions.

Test 1: Job Knowledge Questions

(1) The federal government of the United States is _____.

(A) Totalitarian

(B) Fascist

(C) A republic

(D) Free

(2) How many branches of government does the United States have?

(A) Four

(B) Two

(C) Nine

(D) Three

(3) What is the duty of the three branches of the United States government?

(A) To support the government

(B) To ensure the check and balance of power

(C) To improve the welfare of the people

(D) To enforce laws

(4) It is the responsibility of the _____ to approve judges.

(A) President

(B) Supreme Court

(C) Senate

(D) House of Representatives

(5) The House of Representatives is made up of how many seats?

(A) 50

(B) 51

(C) 435

(D) 278

(6) The additional five delegates and one resident commissioner member of the House of Representatives are _____.

(A) Prior members

(B) Given veto power

(C) Non-voting members

(D) None of the above

(7) The bills for the derivation of revenue come from _____.

(A) The Senate

(B) The House of Representatives

(C) The Senate president

(D) The president

(8) When the president signs a treaty, _____.

(A) It becomes recognized.

(B) It is subject to judiciary approval.

(C) Two-thirds of the Senate must approve the treaty before it becomes recognized.

(D) The treaty cannot be disapproved.

(9) The European colonization of America began in what year?

(A) 1567

(B) 1492

(C) 1789

(D) 1675

(10) Abraham Lincoln became the president of the United States in _____.

(A) 1860

(B) 1870

(C) 1875

(D) 1912

(11) The Jim Crow laws in the late 1800s established_____.

(A) Equality

(B) White supremacy

(C) The Black movement

(D) The abolishment of racial discrimination

(12) What significant event took place in 1929 in American history?

(A) Wall Street crash

(B) The Great Depression

(C) Provision of support for farmers

(D) All of the above

(13) What shifted America's focus from the Cold War in the late 1990s?

(A) The decrease in oil

(B) The Great Depression

(C) The disintegration of the Soviet Union

(D) Inflation in the economy

(14) Which of the following is not true about class distinctions in US society?

(A) Most citizens are middle class.

(B) Just a small number of citizens are middle class.

(C) Seventy-five percent of US citizens are middle class.

(D) The uneducated vote more than the elite.

(15) Rock 'n' roll, rap and jazz originated from which subculture of American society?

(A) Asian American

(B) African American

(C) Hispanic American

(D) Native American

(16) The food Americans eat is _____.

(A) Japanese

(B) Chinese

(C) Italian

(D) All of the above

(17) US foreign policy is meant to _____.

(A) Make the world a better place.

(B) Put America's interests first and protect Americans.

(C) Control power leaders in every country.

(D) Exploit the resources of other nations.

(18) What happens if the citizens of the United States are put second in a negotiation?

(A) The US government may condone it.

(B) The US government will ensure it comes to fruition.

(C) The US government will not condone it.

(D) The US Congress will veto it.

(19) The international relationship between the United States and Asia is built on what model?

(A) Hub and spoke

(B) All-inclusive

(C) Multilateral

(D) Stringent

(20) Why is the United States interested in the Persian Gulf?

(A) There is a need for oil reserves.

(B) The Gulf is beautiful.

(C) It is a political advantage.

(D) It is for cultural reasons.

(21) Which of the following is not a type of nonmilitary aid?

(A) Humanitarian aid

(B) Bilateral development aid

(C) Multilateral economic contributions

(D) National income assistance

(22) The United States is involved in the _____.

(A) Yemen Civil War

(B) Syrian Civil War

(C) Attacks on the Islamic State of Iraq

(D) All of the above

(23) The United States has mutual defense collaborations with which of the following?

(A) Members of NATO

(B) Australia

(C) New Zealand

(D) All of the above

(24) The United States uses which of the following bodies to intervene in international military issues indirectly?

(A) USAID

(B) UN

(C) NATO

(D) WHO

(25) A greater portion of Canada and the Mississippi River area was colonized by the _____.

(A) Dutch

(B) French

(C) Portuguese

(D) Germans

(26) North America is the _____ largest continent in the world.

(A) second

(B) third

(C) fourth

(D) fifth

(27) South America was largely unexplored until _____

(A) The early 1600s

(B) The early 1700s

(C) The early 1800s

(D) The early 1900s

(28) _____explored the Brazilian interior and the Atlantic coast of the South American continent, which led him to the state of Mato Grosso.

(A) Percy Rondo

(B) Cândido Mariano da Silva Rondon

(C) Roberto Carlos

(D) Grosso Martel

(29) What is the name of the British army officer who made the first trip to South America to survey the border between Bolivia and Brazil?

(A) John Baker

(B) Phillip Jude

(C) Brandon Parton

(D) Percy Fawcett

(30) Who set out in 1911 to search for the lost capital of the Incas in the South American wilderness?

(A) Abraham Clinton

(B) Hiram Bingham

(C) Elias Townsend

(D) Henry Ford

(31) The Inca population was approximately _____ at the time of the Spanish conquest.

(A) 9,000,000

(B) 10,000,000

(C) 11,000,000

(D) 12,000,000

(32) What is the name of the tectonic plate in South America?

(A) The South American Plate

(B) The Caribbean Plate

(C) Nazca Plate

(D) All of the above

(33) The primary structure which the US federal government uses to carry out diplomatic functions is _____.

(A) The executive arm

(B) USAID

(C) The Foreign Service

(D) The US embassy

(34) Who is the current director general of the Foreign Service?

(A) James Louis

(B) Barbara Martin

(C) John Jacob

(D) Carol Perez

(35) Between 1975 and 2016, the director general of the Foreign Service was also _____.

(A) The commander in chief

(B) The head of the civil service

(C) The director of the Bureau of Human Resources

(D) The director of welfare

(36) _____ empowers the US secretary of state to send diplomats to other nations through the Foreign Service system.

(A) The Rogers Act

(B) The Consular Act

(C) Article 7 of the United States Constitution

(D) The Foreign Service Act

(37) The Board of the Foreign Service _____.

(A) Counsels interviewees

(B) Counsels the secretary of state on how best to administer the Foreign Service

(C) Created the Board of Examiners of the Foreign Service

(D) Abolished the Rogers Act

(38) The Foreign Agricultural Service was created by the _____.

(A) Department of Agriculture

(B) Department of Horticulture

(C) Department of Diplomacy

(D) Department of Environment

(39) Under the 1946 act, the Board of Foreign Service Personnel was replaced with _____.

(A) The Board of the Foreign Service

(B) Foreign Service ambassadors

(C) The Board of Ambassadors

(D) Consular agents

(40) _____ are senior-ranking officers who recruit new officers for the Foreign Service.

(A) Consular agents

(B) Diplomats in residence

(C) Foreign Service nationals

(D) Junior diplomats

(41) _____ is an electronic machine that accepts and processes data, then produces information.

(A) A keyboard

(B) A monitor

(C) A human

(D) A computer

(42) A complete computer system is made up of _____.

(A) Hardware

(B) Software

(C) Peripheral tools

(D) All of the above

(43) A computer _____.

(A) Can function efficiently without software

(B) Is made up of hardware and software

(C) May not need hardware to function

(D) All of the above.

(44) The four main parts of a general computer include all but which of the following?

(A) The arithmetic logic unit (ALU)

(B) The memory

(C) The light pen

(D) The control unit

(45) A keyboard, mouse, image scanner and camera are _____.

(A) Output devices

(B) Input devices

(C) Software

(D) Control units

(46) Projectors and speakers are _____.

(A) Output devices

(B) Input devices

(C) Software

(D) Control units

(47) _____ includes all the intangible components of the computer.

(A) Software

(B) Hardware

(C) Lightware

(D) Monitor

(48) _____ is the use of specific software to create documents on a computer or desktop.

(A) Text creation

(B) Graphics design

(C) Desktop publishing

(D) Spreadsheet

(49) When you simplify 6/24, the result will be:

(A) 2/7

(B) 3/12

(C) 1/4

(D) 1/24

(50) Janet has 12 hens, and they consume 72 kg of grain every week. Tracy has 20 hens, and they consume 100 kg of grain every week. Whose hens are hungrier?

(A) Tracy's

(B) Janet's

(C) Both girls'

(D) Neither

(51) If A is 5×10^4 and B is 4×10^2, A × B will be:

(A) 20×10^8

(B) 2×10^7

(C) 9×10^6

(D) 20×10^4

(52) $8 - X = 12$. Find X.

(A) 4

(B) -4

(C) 20

(D) 6

(53) The creation of utility or goods and services and the satisfaction of desires or wants, which are remunerated in the form of payment, is _____.

(A) Production

(B) Supply

(C) Demand

(D) Economics

(54) In economics, labor _____.

(A) Is only manual

(B) Is recognized only if it is skilled

(C) Refers to all kinds of effort exerted toward the utility of available resources

(D) Is skilled or unskilled but not manual

(55) Who is in charge of controlling and organizing all the factors of production for the purpose of production?

(A) An entrepreneur

(B) A socialist

(C) A technocrat

(D) A scientist

(56) _____ manage and control public facilities and infrastructures.

(A) Individuals

(B) Administrators

(C) Governments

(D) Banks

(57) Which of the following has the greatest capital size and scope of ownership?

(A) Partnership

(B) Sole proprietorship

(C) Joint-stock company

(D) Dual partnership

(58) Which of the following factors affects the demand for a commodity?

(A) Price

(B) Income

(C) Population size

(D) All of the above

(59) When two items are required in order to give consumers maximal satisfaction, it is called _____ demand.

(A) Complementary

(B) Composite

(C) Competitive

(D) Derived

(60) The United States is a _____ society.

(A) Communist

(B) Capitalist

(C) Socialist

(D) All of the above

Test 1: Situational Judgment Questions

(61) In the federal government, there's a division of labor because _____.

(A) There's a need for checks and balances.

(B) There's a need for productivity.

(C) There will be difficulty in employing non-specialists.

(D) It reduces speed and spending.

(62) Jobs that include a written component require at least ____ people assigned to the task.

(A) One

(B) Two

(C) Three

(D) Four

(63) Which of the following leadership approaches should not be applied in the Foreign Service department?

(A) Persuasion

(B) Voluntary influence

(C) Forceful compulsion

(D) Honorable leadership

(64) In the Foreign Service administration, employees should report to
_____.

(A) One leader

(B) Two leaders

(C) Three leaders

(D) Four leaders

(65) It is _____ to disobey an order from your supervisor if the command does not align with the US Constitution.

(A) Lawful

(B) Unlawful

(C) Dubious

(D) All of the above

(66) A successful administration should have _____ goals.

(A) Minute by minute

(B) Second by second

(C) Quarterly

(D) Unplanned

(67) The commands given to you as a Foreign Service officer _____.

(A) Are always appealing

(B) May be against your religion

(C) Are always in accordance with your political stance

(D) Should not be followed if they are not in favor of your ethnic background

(68) Which of the following is not true about remuneration?

(A) It is a source of motivation.

(B) It should be merit based.

(C) It should be based on sentiment.

(D) It can be either financial or non-financial.

(69) _____ is a major source of conflict and demotivation in organizations.

(A) Reward

(B) Bias

(C) Supervision

(D) Promotion

(70) Without a hierarchy or organogram in an organization, there would be no
_____.

(A) Means of promotion

(B) Anarchy

(C) Disorderliness

(D) All of the above

(71) _____ is/are an aspect of the environment that can affect the morale of workers.

(A) Seats

(B) Tables

(C) Decor

(D) All of the above

(72) Which of the following racial groups is superior?

(A) African

(B) White

(C) Asian

(D) None

(73) _____ is/are not a way of ensuring job security.

(A) Rewards

(B) Promotion

(C) Pension

(D) Increased workload

(74) Foreign Service officers should be _____.

(A) Traditional

(B) Conservative

(C) Partially logical

(D) Innovative

(75) Foreign Service officers of the United States must always put _____ first.

(A) Their children

(B) The nation

(C) Their future

(D) Their state

(76) How should you relate with team members in your place of work?

(A) Focus on building their weaknesses.

(B) Do not bother team members with tasks you can do yourself.

(C) Understand everyone's individuality.

(D) Business should be official and without empathy.

(77) As a diplomat, how should you work with people?

(A) Allow them to see your ideas before they talk.

(B) Gratify their basic desires.

(C) Reduce the rewards.

(D) Trust people based on your instincts.

(78) _____ will help you make a balanced judgment when working with people.

(A) Temperament

(B) Emotional awareness

(C) Self-gratification

(D) Suspicion

(79) When there is a conflict between an Asian American and an African at the embassy, what should you do?

(A) Listen to both parties before passing unprejudiced judgment.

(B) Defend your fellow American citizen after listening to both cases.

(C) Defend the Asian American after listening to both cases.

(D) Speak up for both parties.

(80) If the work environment is tense, what should you do?

(A) Go for a walk and get some fresh air.

(B) Keep your mood upbeat.

(C) React to the situation as it is.

(D) Shout it down.

(81) You are at a negotiation table with sanguine, melancholic, phlegmatic and choleric individuals. Which person is immediately ready to share their deepest thoughts with you?

(A) The sanguine

(B) The melancholic

(C) The phlegmatic

(D) The choleric

(82) Expect to be pushed by a _____ diplomat or boss when there is a task to be done.

(A) Sanguine

(B) Choleric

(C) Melancholic

(D) Phlegmatic

(83) Which of the following temperaments will always seem domineering?

(A) Choleric

(B) Melancholic

(C) Sanguine

(D) Phlegmatic

(84) Melancholics are _____.

(A) Judgmental

(B) Analytical

(C) Depressed

(D) Worriers

(85) While you are working at the embassy, there is a line of people you need to attend to and you see a friend at the back of the line. What should you do?

(A) Explain to those in the line that you want to attend to your friend first.

(B) Call your friend up to the front immediately.

(C) Ignore your friend and ask someone else to attend to them.

(D) Stick to the order of the line until it is your friend's turn.

(86) Which of the following is true about the role of a Foreign Service officer?

(A) It demands knowledge of human behavior.

(B) Officers should be strictly formal without situational context.

(C) It does not require human resource management.

(D) All of the above

(87) When work is divided into units, there is _____.

(A) Chaos and disorder

(B) Delay and unproductivity

(C) Speed and increased productivity

(D) None of the above

(88) Which of the following is necessary in management and administration?

(A) Division of labor

(B) Discipline

(C) Unity of command

(D) All of the above

Test 1: English Expression Questions

Usage of English

Passage 1

(1) <u>The Second Great War</u> has so far been the bloodiest war history ever recorded in history. (2) No fewer than 38 million deaths were recorded before the end of <u>the conflict, most of the victims were innocent civilians</u>. (3) The war involved almost all the nations of the world, but most of it took place in Japan and Europe. (4) The war involved over 50 nations, and its impact will forever be remembered. (5) America's participation in the Second Great War was to end tyranny and promote democracy. <u>(6) Under the leadership of Adolf Hitler, almost every part of Europe in the war had been conquered by the army of Germany.</u>

(7) A lot of people in the new generation wonder how the war began. (8) It started when the German army invaded Poland in 1939. (9) The German army wrought vengeance upon the Jews in any country it invaded. (10) The Germans were also after people whom they considered to be inferior races.

(11) In the Pacific region and Asia, the Japanese military took over nations and islands. (12) December 7, 1941, was when Japanese aircraft rained bombs on Pearl Harbor, Hawaii. (13) The consequence was the United States' participation in World War II.

(14) Historians trace the cause of the Second Great War to World War I, which took place between 1914 and 1918. (15) When America participated in World War I, it was simply to ensure that the world was a better place and democracy thrived. (16) This was the vision of President Woodrow Wilson, who was president from 1913 to 1921. (17) Most people had thought the peace treaties would be the ultimate solution, but the unallayed grievances culminated in the Second Great War.

(18) When Germany and its allies were vanquished in World War I, they were asked to yield one-sixth of all its territories and to pay a reparation fee <u>(payment that countries pay as compensation after being defeated in a war)</u>. (19) Other forms of penalties were <u>additionally</u> meted out to Germany. (20) Some of these penalties included the disarmament of their military forces and restrictions.

(89) Another word for the underlined item in sentence 1 is _____.

(A) The Second War

(B) World War II

(C) The Second Conflict

(D) The Last Fight

(90) Which of the following sentence constructions is preferable for sentence 2?

(A) The conflict and most of the victims were innocent citizens

(B) The conflict and most of the victims were innocent citizens

(C) The conflict and most, of the victims were innocent citizens

(D) The conflict and most of the victims, were innocent citizens

(91) Which part of sentence 6 should be changed?

(A) No change

(B) Almost every part of Europe in the war had been conquered by the army of Germany.

(C) Under the leadership

(D) Adolf Hitler

(92) How can sentence 18 be revised?

(A) No change.

(B) Remove the parentheses.

(C) Include a comma.

(D) Remove the sentence.

(93) What role does the underlined item in sentence 19 play?

(A) It adds more information.

(B) It does not play any role.

(C) It contradicts the other sentences.

(D) It decreases the meaning of the sentence.

Sentence Selection:

(94) Choose the sentence that is most suitable for standard written English.

(A) The manager owes much of his performance due to having a variety of experts in the company.

(B) The manager owes much of his performance resulting from having a variety of experts in the company.

(C) The manager owes much of his performance to a variety of experts in the company.

(D) The manager owes much of his performance to its experts that are in varieties in the company.

(95) Choose the sentence that is most suitable for standard written English.

(A) We met the girl three days ago

(B) We met the girl for three days ago

(C) We met the girl after three days ago

(D) We met the girl three days ago.

(96) Choose the sentence that is most suitable for standard written English.

(A) All the other rooms were not organized.

(B) All other rooms were not well organized

(C) All other rooms were not organized in the most beautiful way

(D) All other rooms were not organized properly.

Sentence Correction I

For each sentence, choose the underlined word(s) that contain an error or choose the answer option that indicates no error in the sentence.

(97) Citizens of <u>America a country with great beauty</u>, should <u>be proud</u> of <u>their country.</u>

(A) No errors

(B) America a country with great beauty

(C) be proud

(D) their country

(98) The Foreign Service officer as well as his children are traveling tomorrow.

(A) No errors

(B) The Foreign

(C) as well as

(D) are

(99) I came early to the workshop and found out that the number of US officials was around fifty.

(A) No errors

(B) early to

(C) of US officials

(D) was

Sentence Correction II

For each sentence, choose the word that should replace the underlined word(s) to correct the sentence, or identify if there are no errors.

(100) Haven't you heard that the new president of *Time* magazine is <u>mine</u> father?

(A) No errors

(B) My

(C) We're

(D) Were

(101) When I went to the restaurant, I bought chicken and rice, which <u>have always been</u> my favorite food.

(A) No errors

(B) Is

(C) Are

(D) Were

Paragraph Organization

(102) Choose the clearest and most organized sentence arrangement.

Sentence 1: Many countries are trying to control the rate at which the ozone layer is depleting.

Sentence 2: The atmosphere is grouped into different layers—troposphere, stratosphere, mesosphere, thermosphere and exosphere.

Sentence 3: The depletion of the ozone layer has known and unknown harmful effects.

Sentence 4: The ozone layer is found in the stratosphere, which is 10 km and 80 km from the ground surface, and the greatest concentration is at 25 km from the ground.

(A) 1, 2, 3, 4

(B) 1, 2, 4, 3

(C) 2, 4, 3, 1

(D) 2, 4, 1, 3

(103) Choose the clearest and most organized sentence arrangement.

Sentence 1: A computer is an electronic system, which is used for collecting, storing and producing information.

Sentence 2: Computers should be used cautiously because of their negative aspects.

Sentence 3: The history of computers can be traced to the creation of automated calculation devices.

Sentence 4: There are different classifications of computers.

(A) 1, 2, 3, 4

(B) 1, 3, 4, 2

(C) 3, 1, 4, 2

(D) 4, 3, 2, 1

(104) Choose the clearest and most organized sentence arrangement.

Sentence 1: In many nations, the trafficking of drugs is a severe offense that incurs severe penalties.

Sentence 2: Drug trafficking has various debilitating effects on US society.

Sentence 3: Drug trafficking is a worldwide unlawful trade that involves the production and distribution of contraband drugs.

Sentence 4: Drug trafficking can be eradicated through enlightenment campaigns and stringent policies that prohibit drug abuse.

(A) 1, 2, 3, 4

(B) 1, 3, 4, 2

(C) 2, 3, 4, 1

(D) 3, 1, 2, 4

(105) Choose the clearest and most organized sentence arrangement.

Sentence 1: Animals do not have chlorophyll and cannot produce their own food.

Sentence 2: Plants can produce their own food, then use it for survival.

Sentence 3: Living things are grouped into two main categories: plants and animals.

Sentence 4: Living things are animate creatures or things that have life.

(A) 1, 2, 3, 4

(B) 2, 3, 1, 4

(C) 3, 1, 2, 4

(D) 4, 3, 2, 1

(106) Choose the clearest and most organized sentence arrangement.

Sentence 1: Having a flat tire and no idea how to change it can lead to frustration.

Sentence 2: Use a screwdriver to take off the wheel cover.

Sentence 3: Jack the vehicle up.

Sentence 4: Use bricks or wedges to chock the wheel.

(A) 1, 2, 3, 4

(B) 1, 2, 4, 3

(C) 1, 4, 3, 2

(D) 2, 1, 4, 3

Paragraph Revision

Read these sentences and then answer the questions that follow.

Sentence 1: In a society that practices a mixed economy, the government interferes in the public market to provide public utilities, such as national defense and infrastructure.

Sentence 2: The federal government also intervenes in the public market through the distribution of wealth among _our_ countrymen for sociocultural or political reasons.

Sentence 3: Government also intervenes because of external factors which exist when there is a difference between private costs and social costs.

Sentence 4: The distribution of wealth involves the support of commodities for agricultural producers, maintenance of income and provision of health care for families that are low-income earners.

(107) The writer finds out that this sentence has been omitted from the above paragraph: "For instance, car owners take the burden of what the emissions cost." The insertion of this sentence would be most suitable after which sentence?

(A) Sentence 1

(B) Sentence 2

(C) Sentence 3

(D) Sentence 4

(108) Choose the alternative that will most suitably replace the underlined item in sentence 2.

(A) it's

(B) its

(C) yours

(D) their

Word Selection.

(109) The man and _____ traveled yesterday.

(A) me

(B) them

(C) I

(D) us

(110) _____ house is being built.

(A) Yours

(B) Your's

(C) Your

(D) Yourses

(111) She saw _____ on her way to church.

(A) she

(B) they

(C) I

(D) her

(112) He is lying _____ the bench.

(A) with

(B) on

(C) inside

(D) in

(113) They looked at me _____ anger.

(A) inside

(B) with

(C) by

(D) from

(114) A naming word is known as _____.

(A) An adjective

(B) A preposition

(C) A noun

(D) An adverb

(115) I have many _____.

(A) Sherps

(B) Sheep

(C) Sheeps'

(D) Sheep's

(116) A pair of glasses _____ missing.

(A) Are

(B) Is

(C) Were

(D) Had

(117) The women, as well as the man, _____ visiting.

(A) Are

(B) Is

(C) Was

(D) Wered

(118) Mathematics _____ my favorite subject.

(A) Are

(B) Were

(C) Is

(D) Have been

(119) A number of students _____ arrived.

(A) Has

(B) Have

(C) Haved

(D) Hased

(120) One-quarter of the building _____ been completed.

(A) Haved

(B) Has

(C) Were

(D) Is

(121) Twenty thousand dollars _____ much.

(A) Were

(B) Are

(C) Is

(D) Have

(122) Neither Bryan nor the men _____ her whereabouts.

(A) Knows

(B) Know

(C) Knowed

(D) Know's

(123) _____ high time we left this place.

(A) It's

(B) It

(C) Its'

(D) Its

(124) Which of the following adjectives is in the comparative form?

(A) Tallest

(B) Tall

(C) Taller

(D) Tallest

(125) The parts of speech concerned with describing nouns or pronouns are _____

(A) Pronouns

(B) Adjectives

(C) Interjections

(D) Conjunctions

(126) Which of the following is not a part of speech?

(A) Adverb

(B) Adjective

(C) Noun clause

(D) Noun

(127) My glasses _____ missing.

(A) Is

(B) Are

(C) Has

(D) Would

(128) When the results were released, the students were on cloud nine, meaning _____.

(A) The students were angry.

(B) The students were afraid.

(C) The students were happy.

(D) The students were proud.

(129) From all indications, he has his back against the wall. What does this mean?

(A) He is a painter.

(B) He is in a hard situation.

(C) He likes enjoying himself.

(D) He wants to be serious in life.

(130) Bryan is head over heels in love with Mary. What does this mean?

(A) Bryan loves Mary.

(B) Bryan hates Mary.

(C) Bryan does not know Mary.

(D) Bryan displeases Mary.

(131) The man accused his wife of upsetting his applecart. What does this mean?

(A) The wife made his plans succeed.

(B) The wife made his plans fail.

(C) The wife made his plans better.

(D) The wife stole his apples.

(132) She was up in arms because of her father's decision to stop her from going to school any longer. What does this mean?

(A) She was happy.

(B) She was not happy.

(C) She was indifferent.

(D) She was amazed.

(133) The woman had to bend over backward to stop her husband from marrying another woman. What does this mean?

(A) The woman had to please her husband.

(B) The woman displeased her husband.

(C) The woman loves yoga.

(D) The woman stopped loving her husband.

(134) The workers made no bones about their unpaid salaries. What does this mean?

(A) The workers expressed their feelings.

(B) The workers fought one another.

(C) The workers quit.

(D) The workers got a bonus.

(135) The doctor broke new ground last year. What does this mean?

(A) The doctor achieved something last year.

(B) The doctor saw something new on the ground.

(C) The doctor went to a new ground.

(D) The doctor saw a new ground.

(136) The lecturer likes saying one thing and then another in the same breath. What does this mean?

(A) The lecturer likes breathing.

(B) The lecturer likes making contradictory statements.

(C) The lecturer likes speaking.

(D) The lecturer likes the audience.

(137) Peter burns the candle at both ends. What does this mean?

(A) Peter loves candles.

(B) Peter is ill.

(C) Peter works hard.

(D) Peter is lazy.

(138) When he discovered that he was late for the meeting, he started working against the clock. What does this mean?

(A) He lost his clock.

(B) He was trying to make up for lost time.

(C) He worked for a company named Clock.

(D) He was lazy.

(139) Storytelling is helpful during communication because _____.

(A) Humans love pleasure.

(B) Humans like being stressed out.

(C) The story is real.

(D) The story is imagined.

(140) Which of the following places is not suitable for sharing exclusive information?

(A) Marketplace

(B) Office space

(C) Veranda

(D) Garden

(141) Which of the following is not a negative nonverbal communication?

(A) Slouching

(B) Frowning

(C) Silence

(D) Happiness

(142) A monotone voice in communication should be avoided because
_____.

(A) It is appealing to the ear.

(B) It is unappealing to the ear.

(C) It helps one improve one's hearing ability.

(D) It is good for the ear.

(143) All except _____ are qualities of effective speakers.

(A) Confidence

(B) Passion

(C) Directness

(D) Procrastinating

(144) Which of the following is not a reason for taking a deep breath before continuing to speak?

(A) It helps you stay steady while communicating.

(B) It helps you gain balance.

(C) It helps you take a glimpse of your notes.

(D) It helps you hear better.

(145) Effective speakers are known to be concise because _____.

(A) An audience often does not have a long attention span.

(B) An audience likes hearing stories.

(C) An audience likes entertainment.

(D) An audience likes amusing one another.

(146) Which of the following is not a reason to take a pause during communication?

(A) To give the listener an opportunity to pay attention to what is coming next

(B) To give the listener the opportunity to attend to other issues or activities

(C) To give listeners some time to think about what was just said

(D) To enable your words to be more compelling

(147) Which of the following is not a reason for making eye contact with your audience?

(A) To show you are conceited

(B) To show you are confident

(C) To show you are honorable

(D) To show you are truthful

(148) Communicating effectively as a Foreign Service officer includes all of the following except _____.

(A) Ensuring the environment is ideal

(B) Setting up communications

(C) Watching your speech

(D) Using vague vocabulary

(149) All except _____ are qualities of an effective speaker.

(A) Confidence

(B) Passion

(C) Conciseness

(D) Shyness

(150) When a speaker speaks effectively, the audience becomes _____ .

(A) Eager to hear more

(B) Lazy

(C) Uninterested

(D) Confused

(151) An environment filled with noise and disorderliness will _____

(A) Distort the flow of communication

(B) Help promote understanding between both parties

(C) Help create a better understanding

(D) Make the communication better

(152) Frowning or raising your brow may _____

(A) Make the audience love you

(B) Send a negative message to your audience

(C) Make you more popular

(D) Make the conversation interesting

(153) Speakers should be _____

(A) Vague

(B) Concise

(C) Redundant

(D) Time consuming

Test 1: Essay Question

College sports are becoming more popular in the United States. An organization like the National Collegiate Athletic Association (NCAA) generates massive revenue from different sporting activities every year. The huge amount of money generated has led to debates about whether college athletes should be paid. What is your take on this debate?

Test 1: Job Knowledge Answers and Explanations

(1) (C) A republic.

A republic allows people to exercise power individually or through representatives. The federal government of the United States is a republic. It is made of 50 states, 14 independent territories and islands, one federal district and 15 departments.

(2) (D) Three.

The three branches of the United States government are the legislature, the executive and the judiciary.

(3) (B) To ensure the check and balance of power.

The duty of the three branches is to ensure there are checks and balances within the US government. The United States government is neither an authoritarian nor a monarchical government. It practices a democratic system of government.

(4) (B) Supreme Court.

It is the duty of the Supreme Court to approve judges. It is the president's job to nominate judges. This is an act of checks and balances.

(5) (C) 435.

The House of Representatives is made of 435 seats, each of which represents a district in the United States. The proportion of representatives per state is based on the population of the state. A state has to have at least one representative. The representatives serve two years.

(6) (C) Non-voting members.

Aside from the 435 members who are eligible for voting, there are also six members who do not vote. These additional members are five delegates and one resident commissioner.

(7) (B) The House of Representatives.

The bills for the derivation of revenue come from the House of Representatives. All legislation must have the consent of both chambers and receive the signature of the president before it can become law.

(8) (C) Two-thirds of the Senate must approve the treaty before it becomes recognized.

The president may undertake diplomatic negotiations and signing of treaties. Two-thirds of the Senate must approve these before they become recognized. The president is the commander in chief of the armed forces, the ceremonial head (head of state) and the chief executive (head of government).

(9) (B) 1492.

The colonization of America by the Europeans began in 1492 when Christopher Columbus arrived on the continent.

(10) (A) 1860.

Abraham Lincoln became president in 1860. He came to office with the intention of abolishing slavery and was vehemently opposed. As a result of his election, seven states in the South decided to form the Confederate States of America.

(11) (B) White supremacy.

In the late 1800s, Southern leaders got back to power in government and created laws that favored discrimination. They enacted the Jim Crow laws, which established White supremacy. There was also discrimination against African Americans and poor Whites.

(12) (D) All of the above.

The United States suffered a crash on Wall Street in 1929. That caused the Great Depression, a period of economic hardship that lasted almost a decade. During this era, President Franklin Roosevelt enacted the New Deal, which supported farmers and established the Social Security program.

(13) (C) The disintegration of the Soviet Union.

A Cold War emerged between the United States and the Soviets after World War II. The basis of the Cold War was a fight to become the world's first superpower. The Cold War suffered a sociopolitical death when the Soviet Union dissolved in 1991. At the cessation of the Cold War, much of America's focus changed to conflicts in the Middle East.

(14) (D) The uneducated vote more than the elite.

United States society is made up of class distinctions, although most individuals or homes identify themselves as middle class. Education affects the voting behavior of Americans. The elite or educated tend to vote more than the less educated. Those who earn more have access to better health care, education and social facilities. On average, most employed Americans work 42.9 hours a week.

(15) (B) African American.

Segregation in American society led to subcultures and was responsible for the creation of Chinatowns, Harlem and the African American society. The United States owes much of its musical creativity to African Americans, who produced various genres of music like rock 'n' roll, jazz, rap and the blues.

(16) (D) All of the above.

The United States has a diverse cuisine due to its long history of immigration and diverse ethnic makeup. There is Japanese, Thai, Chinese and Italian cuisine, among many more. The type of food an American household consumes largely depends on family background.

(17) (B) Put America's interests first and protect Americans.

US foreign policy is meant to control exports, stop the proliferation of nuclear weapons, increase business communication with nations and protect Americans and the country's investments in other countries. It is meant to put America's interests first and protect Americans. The United States is often considered the watchdog of the world.

(18) (C) The US government will not condone it.

It is not in the foreign policy of the United States to compulsorily participate in all agreements that the international community agrees to abide by. If it does not suit the interest of the United States, then the United States is not obligated to condone such agreements.

(19) (A) Hub and spoke.

The international relationship between the United States and Asia is built on a hub and spoke model, which uses bilateral agreements between individual nations and the United States.

(20) (A) There is a need for oil reserves.

About two-thirds of the world's oil reserves are believed to be in the Persian Gulf. During World War II, the United States identified its interest in this region. Several decades later, the US enacted Jimmy Carter's doctrine, which made it clear that when necessary, the United States would use military force to secure its national interest in the Persian Gulf area.

(21) (D) National income assistance.

This is not a type of nonmilitary aid. The United States offers foreign aid to nations and institutions all over the world. Foreign aid is a key aspect of the State Department's international relations. As of 2014, the budget for international affairs was $49 billion. Nonmilitary aid is classified into four categories: humanitarian aid, bilateral development aid, multilateral economic contributions and economic assistance. These all align with US goals.

(22) (D) All of the above.

In 2016, the United States started military attacks on the Islamic State of Iraq, Al-Qaeda and the Levant. It is involved in the Yemen Civil War and the Syrian Civil War. The naval base at Guantanamo Bay contains what the United States has declared to be unlawful combatants.

(23) (D) All of the above.

The US government has mutual defense agreements with members of NATO, Australia, New Zealand and others. The United States is also in a mutual defense agreement with South America, the Caribbean and Central America. This agreement is based on the Inter-American Treaty of Reciprocal Assistance.

(24) (C) NATO.

Sometimes the United States acts indirectly on international issues but through NATO. This indirect intervention can be seen in NATO's role in the attacking of Yugoslavia, Afghanistan, Bosnia and Herzegovina. However, the US military often prefers to work unilaterally or through ad hoc coalitions, as seen in the 2003 operations in Iraq.

(25) (B) French.

The French colonized a large part of Canada and the Mississippi River area.

(26) (B) Third.

North America lies between the Arctic Circle and the Tropic of Cancer, making it the third-largest continent in the world. Lying within 500 miles (800 kilometers) of both the North Pole and the equator, it extends more than 5,000 miles (8,000 kilometers).

(27) (D) The early 1900s.

South America was largely unexplored as of the early 1900s. For transportation and commerce, it relied on waterways, with few roads connecting major cities.

(28) (B) Cândido Mariano da Silva Rondon.

Cândido Mariano da Silva Rondon was one of the greatest explorers in South America. He explored the Brazilian interior and the Atlantic coast of the continent, eventually leading him to the state of Mato Grosso, where he set out to build a telegraph line and a road to Rio de Janeiro.

(29) (D) Percy Fawcett.

British army officer Percy Fawcett made his first trip to South America, where he surveyed the border between Bolivia and Brazil after Cândido Mariano da Silva Rondon completed the Brazilian telegraph line.

(30) (B) Hiram Bingham.

Hiram Bingham set out in 1911 to search for the lost capital of the Incas in the South American wilderness.

(31) (D) 12,000,000.

The Inca population was approximately 12,000 people at the time of the Spanish conquest, with its domain stretching to the northern border of Ecuador.

(32) (D) All of the above.

There are three plates in South America: the South American Plate, the Caribbean Plate and the Nazca Plate, which consists of the South Pacific Ocean. At 6.87 million square miles, it is the fourth-largest continent in the world.

(33) (C) The Foreign Service.

The Foreign Service is the primary structure through which the US federal government carries out diplomatic functions. The Foreign Service operates under the auspices of the US Department of State. It is estimated that there are about 13,000 skilled workers who are enforcing the foreign policies of the United States and supporting citizens of the United States who are living abroad.

(34) (D) Carol Perez.

The Foreign Service is superintended by a director general. Currently, Carol Perez is the director general of the Foreign Service. The position of the director general of the Foreign Service is appointed by the president with the suggestion and approval of the Senate.

(35) (C) The director of the Bureau of Human Resources.

From November 23, 1975, until October 2, 2016, the director general was also the director of the Bureau of Human Resources. Being the superintendent of the bureau, the rank of the director general was the same as the assistant secretary of state. Currently, both positions—director general of the Foreign Service and director of the Bureau of Human Resources—are not held by the same person.

(36) (A) The Rogers Act.

The Foreign Service was formed in 1924 through the Rogers Act. It was made to be a single administrative unit that combines all diplomatic and consular services as one. The Rogers Act states that it is through the Foreign Service system that the US secretary of state sends diplomats to other nations.

(37) (B) Counsels the secretary of state on how best to administer the Foreign Service.

The Rogers Act was the progenitor of the Board of the Foreign Service, which was to counsel the secretary of state on how best to administer the Foreign Service. The Rogers Act also created the Board of Examiners of the Foreign Service for the administration of Foreign Service examinations.

(38) (A) Department of Agriculture.

The Foreign Agricultural Service was established by the Department of Agriculture in 1930. This was an agricultural extension of the Foreign Service. The civil servants working in the agricultural and commercial extensions were already diplomats, but they were not Foreign Service officers until the legislation was passed.

(39) (A) The Board of the Foreign Service.

Under the 1946 act, the Board of Foreign Service Personnel was replaced with the Board of the Foreign Service. The former was meant to administer the structure of promotions, while the latter was broader in scope since it was in charge of the whole personnel structure. The 1946 act was modeled on the US Army, as it started the up-or-out promotion system.

(40) (B) Diplomats in residence.

Diplomats in residence are senior-ranking officers who recruit new officers for the Foreign Service. They are found in assigned locations and have honorary positions in universities that are in the locality. Like all other Foreign Service officers, they are diplomats meant to carry out diplomatic functions without partiality or personal interest.

(41) (D) A computer.

A computer is an electronic machine that accepts and processes data, then produces information. It is programmed to automatically work out logical operations. A complete computer system is made up of hardware, software or operating system and peripheral tools. A computer may function as a unit or a network.

(42) (D) All of the above.

A complete computer system is made up of hardware, software or operating system and peripheral tools.

(43) (B) Is made up of hardware and software.

A complete computer system is made up of hardware, software or operating system and peripheral tools.

(44) (C) The light pen.

A computer that serves general use has four main parts: the arithmetic logic unit (ALU), the input and output devices, the memory and the control unit. These parts are interconnected. The light pen is a peripheral component of a computer. It is not one of the most essential parts.

(45) (B) Input devices.

Input devices send data to the computer. The CPU processes the data before it is produced as information through the output device. Examples of input devices are a keyboard, mouse, image scanner, camera, joystick, light pen, touch screen, microphone and trackball. They complement the other main parts of the computer, or arithmetic logic unit (ALU), the output devices, the memory and the control unit.

(46) (A) Output devices.

Output devices are used to produce information after the input device has sent data for the CPU to process. Examples of output devices are a monitor, printer, video card, projector and speaker.

(47) (A) Software.

Software includes the intangible components of a computer. Examples are protocols, programs, data, etc. Software also includes computer-encoded instructions or information, such as libraries, computer programs, digital media or online documentation.

Software is classified into system and application software. System software includes Unix, BSD, Linux, DOS, Mackintosh operating system and Microsoft Windows. Application software includes database management, desktop publishing, spreadsheet, internet access, graphics, audio and games.

(48) (C) Desktop publishing.

Desktop publishing is the use of specific software to create documents on a computer or desktop. It is used in producing text and images. It helps businesses and individuals publish content, such as brochures, books, flyers and magazines. When you use desktop publishing software to create content, you have more control over the typography, the design and the layout.

(49) (C) 1/4.

The answer to this question is derived from the rules of simplification, which involves division.

The best number to use for the division is the highest common factor of 6 and 24, which is 6. Therefore:

6 divided by 6 = 1

24 divided by 6 = 4

The answer is: 1/4.

(50) (A) Tracy's.

Janet's ratio = 12:72. To get the precise rate, simplify the ratio. Divide the numerator and denominator by 12. The result will be 1:6.

Tracy's ratio = 20:100. But to get the precise rate, simplify the ratio. Divide the numerator and denominator by 20. The result will be 1:5.

This means that Janet's hens eat 6 kg, and Tracy's hens eat 5 kg. Janet's hens are hungrier.

(51) (B) 2×10^7.

First, multiply the two whole numbers:

$5 \times 4 = 20$

Then $10^4 \times 10^2 = 10^6$. (Don't multiply the powers. Instead, add them.)

$= 20 \times 10^6$

However, in standard form, the first part (20) should not be more than 1–10. Therefore:

$2 \times 10 \times 10^6$

$= 2 \times 10^7$

(52) (B) -4.

Subtract 8 from both sides to make X stand alone.

$8 - 8 - X = 12 - 8$

$-X = 4$

Since we are looking for X, not -X, divide both sides by -1. The calculation will be:

$-X/-1 = 4/-1$

The value of X is -4.

(53) (A) Production.

Production is the creation of utility or goods and services and the satisfaction of desires or wants, which are remunerated in the form of payment. It is the utilization of specific factors of production for the creation of these goods and services. The factors of production are land, labor, capital and enterprise.

(54) (C) Refers to all kinds of effort exerted toward the utility of available resources.

Labor refers to all kinds of effort exerted toward the utilization of available resources for production. Labor can be mental, manual, skilled or unskilled and is often rewarded after the completion of a task. Some economists prefer to call labor the prime mover because it is the initiator of all productive plans. Without labor, all other processes of production become fallow.

(55) (A) An entrepreneur.

An entrepreneur is in charge of controlling and organizing all the factors of production for the purpose of production. Entrepreneurs may be directors, managers or owners of public or private enterprises. They bear the risks involved in the production and distribution of goods and services.

(56) (C) Government.

The government manages and controls public facilities and infrastructures.

(57) (C) Joint-stock company.

A joint-stock company has a greater capital size and a wider scope of ownership than a sole proprietorship or partnership. Many people can buy the organization's shares as a form of investment. Because of their capital size and rate of productivity, joint-stock companies have a great impact on the economy of the United States. Investors or shareholders in joint-stock companies enjoy the advantage of limited liability and continuity that these companies offer.

(58) (D) All of the above.

In economics, demand is the quantity of goods and services consumers are willing and have the capacity to buy at a defined price and time. Demand is not always static. It is affected by factors such as the price of the goods and services, the price of complementary and competing goods and services, income, population size, changes in preferences of consumers, environmental and social conditions and government policies.

(59) (A) Complementary.

There are five general classifications of demand—competitive demand, derived demand, complementary or joint demand, composite demand and independent demand. When two items are demanded because they are needed before they can give consumers maximal satisfaction, then both items are complementarily demanded. Examples are bread and butter, cereal and milk, etc.

(60) (B) Capitalist.

The United States is a capitalist society. Capitalism is a market system that requires private control of properties. In a capitalist state, there is a free enterprise that is regulated by governmental agencies. Private owners have the freedom to explore opportunities within the capacity of their capital. A capitalist state is highly competitive, and the primary pursuit is to make a profit.

Test 1: Situational Judgment Answers and Explanations

(61) (B) The need for productivity.

Henri Foyal believed that when work is divided into units, there is greater productivity and quality of output. When there is an appropriate division of work, there is efficiency, speed and order. That is why there is a division of labor in the federal government.

(62) (C) Three.

Jobs with a written component require that there should be an assigned writer and at least two editors. As a Foreign Service officer, you should be ready to divide tasks among team members. Collaboration is the easiest, fastest and most productive way of dealing with challenges.

(63) (C) Forceful compulsion.

Respectable leadership and not forceful compulsion is what every managing body does to make workers find their job enjoyable.

(64) (A) One leader.

Every employee or Foreign Service officer should report to just one boss. A multiplicity of instructions from different bosses often results in confusion and conflict. This is called disunity in command.

(65) (A) Lawful.

It is lawful to disobey an order from your supervisor if the command does not align with the US Constitution. Whatever decisions you make in the Foreign Service must be in alignment with the Constitution. This is called unity of command.

(66) (C) Quarterly.

A successful administration should have quarterly goals. The goals must be specific, measurable, attainable, relevant to making an impact in the US economy and time bound. Everyone in your department should be pursuing the same or similar goals. This is called unity of direction.

(67) (B) May be against your religion.

The command given may not be pleasing to you due to your religion, personal beliefs, political stance or ethnic background. Regardless, you should comply with the order. It is wrong and unconstitutional to put your personal interest above your nation.

(68) (C) It should be based on sentiment.

This is not true. Remuneration should be merit based, not based on sentiment. Rewards can be either financial or non-financial. When leading a team, never expect that your employees' passion for service is all they need to get the task done. Remuneration is a source of motivation in every organization and this includes the Foreign Service.

(69) (B) Bias.

Ethnic, religious or personal biases are major sources of conflict that demotivate workers. Henri Fayol stated that the central body or management should maintain a neutral stance.

(70) (A) Means of promotion.

Fayol stipulated the need for a hierarchy that starts at the top and flow to the bottom. Every officer should have direct access to his or her superiors. This is needed for the transfer of information, promotion of officers and specialization in roles.

(71) (D) All of the above.

The workplace environment and atmosphere must be conducive to efficiency. Seats, tables, decor and every aspect of the work environment should boost the morale of officers. When there is no orderliness, frustration, unproductivity and chaos will result.

(72) (D) None.

Some people still practice White supremacy. They believe people with White skin color are superior to people from other races, and they transfer this misconception to the workplace. This is wrong. No race is superior. We are all equal. In the workplace, you should treat everyone with equality. There should be no racial, gender, religious or personal biases. No employee or customer should face discrimination.

(73) (D) Increased workload.

An increased workload will lead to stress, and nobody wants to stay long in a place where there is stress. People tend to work better if there is stability in the workplace. If the administration offers job security, fewer penalties and an enabling environment, employees will feel safe investing their time and effort.

(74) (D) Innovative.

As a Foreign Service officer, you have to take an innovative approach toward problem-solving. Do not be too traditional or conservative in your methodologies. Be open to new ideas. Stay process minded, but be results oriented. Authorities should encourage initiative. When workers see that their initiatives are recognized, they will do more.

(75) (B) The nation.

United States Foreign officers must always put their nation (the United States) first.

(76) (C) Understand everyone's individuality.
Team members must understand everyone's individuality. This includes basic elements like people's temperaments, strengths, weaknesses, motivations and perspectives. When team members understand one another, then it will be easy for them to complete tasks. They must understand the vision and mission, then be technically fit for the task.

(77) (B) Gratify their basic desires.

Motivation is a key factor in the workplace. Foreign Service officers who are motivated through monetary rewards or other forms of rewards tend to be more productive. Humans are wired to stake their time and efforts on things that will gratify their basic desires.

(78) (B) Emotional awareness.

To have a successful career in the Foreign Service, you must master the art of emotional awareness. For effective collaboration, you must consider people's emotions and seek to understand the people you are working with.

(79) (A) Listen to both parties before passing unprejudiced judgment.

It is important to see crises in the workplace as situations that cannot be totally avoided. Be diplomatic, impartial and equitable when resolving conflicts. Listen to all sides before passing unprejudiced judgment. Never judge a case based on racial sentiments.

(80) (B) Keep your mood upbeat.

Keep your mood lively and upbeat when relating to people. This is because moods are contagious. A positive mood will bring out the best in those around you. Instead of being tense or antagonistic, be cheerful and optimistic to make others feel relaxed and ready to work for the good of the organization.

(81) (A) The sanguine.

Sanguines are extroverts. People in this category like to go out. They derive joy in relating with people. They relish teamwork and fellowship. Their enthusiasm is contagious. This quality is what makes you feel relaxed when you are with them. Sanguines do not know how to hide their feelings, and that is why people tend to trust them in relationships.

(82) (B) Choleric.

Cholerics are goal-driven people who set goals and do all they can to achieve them. They have a positive attitude toward their plans and are not discouraged even when they are facing obstacles. When you see someone who is very practical about life and is focused on getting desired results, then you have met a choleric.

(83) (A) Choleric.

Cholerics are very assertive with their decisions. This attitude makes them seem domineering. They are quick in carrying out what is on their mind, and they take risks. Cholerics like to be in charge. Therefore, they do not mind making decisions for others.

(84) (D) Worriers.

Melancholics are worriers and are often very cautious when making decisions. They are often obsessed with details and are most times seen as perfectionists. They tend to operate by the book. Melancholics are introverted, analytical, logical and great planners. They often regret past mistakes and worry about what the future holds.

(85) (D) Stick to the order of the line until it is your friend's turn.

Stick with the order of the line until it is your friend's turn. This is professional ethics. There should be no partiality when working. Everyone should be treated equally.

(86) (A) It demands knowledge of human behavior.

The job of a Foreign Service officer demands an understanding of human psychology and behavior. You should be able to manage situations wisely. The Foreign Service officer role requires human resource management skills. Officers need to be contextual and not strictly formal in their dealing with people. Every officer should follow Henri Fayol's principles of management.

(87) (C) Speed and increased productivity.

Henri Foyal said that when work is divided into units, there is greater speed, productivity and quality of output. When there is an appropriate division of work, there is efficiency, speed and order.

(88) (D) All of the above.

Division of labor, discipline and unity of command are all necessary in management and administration.

Test 1: English Expressions Answers and Explanations

(89) (B) World War II.

World War II is a synonym for the Second Great War. The Second Conflict or the Last Fight will not convey the intended meaning. Besides, no one knows if that will be the last fight.

(90) (A) The conflict and most of the victims were innocent citizens.

The comma is meant to ensure fluency in a text. It should not be used in place of a period.

(91) (B) Almost every part of Europe in the war had been conquered by the army of Germany.

This sentence is in the passive voice. The best way to write this sentence is in the active voice. That is, the subject of the verb should precede the object of the action.

(92) (A) No change.

The parentheses are used to show that additional content has been included in the original text. They are used to make side comments. Ellipses are also used to show that there is discontinuity from the main thought.

(93) (A) It adds more information.

Additionally is an adverb. Adverbs modify the action of a verb, the description of an adjective or another adverb. They often end in *-ly*, *-wise*, or *-ward*. Examples are *slowly, happily, angrily, clockwise, backward*. Other examples of adverbs that do not take inflections are *however, furthermore, very, only* and *since,* among others.

(94) (C) The manager owes much of his performance to a variety of experts in the company.

This option is more concise than the other options. It briefly presents the message without altering the meaning. It is clear and unambiguous. Wordiness and redundancy should be avoided when writing standard English. Standard written English demands clarity.

(95) (D) We met the girl three days ago.

A period should be placed at the end of a sentence. Option D is the only option with a period. Also, Options B and C contain grammatical errors.

(96) (A) All the other rooms were not organized.

This option is more concise than the other options. It briefly presents the message without altering the meaning. It is clear and unambiguous. Use a period at the end of every sentence. Always use the definite article *the* when you're specific about an item.

(97) (B) America a country with great beauty.

The phrase *a country with great beauty* is an appositive to *America*. This means that the phrase is adding more information to *America*. It is describing America. An appositive is sometimes called a zero-relative clause because it does not contain the relative pronoun *who, which, that, whose, where, when,* etc.

Therefore, there need to be commas to separate the appositive from the item that is being described.

(98) (D) Are.

Ignore words that look like the coordinator *and*. They are called pseudo coordinators, and you should not associate the combinatory or pluralizing function of *and* to them unless the subject is plural. This includes *as well as, in addition to, in the company of, alongside, in conjunction with*, etc. They should not affect the nature of the verb. In this case, the subject is singular—*Foreign Officer*—and therefore the plural verb *are* is incorrect.

(99) (A) No errors.

There is no error in this sentence.

(100) (B) My.

The correct sentence should read: *Haven't you heard that the president of Time magazine is my father?* The question is on pronoun case. The sentence requires the use of a possessive pronoun. Possessive pronouns are *his, her, its, my, mine, their, theirs, your, yours, our* and *ours*. They are used to show ownership. Whenever *mine* is used, there should not be a qualified noun in front of it.

(101) (B) Is.

The correct sentence should read: *When I went to the restaurant, I bought chicken and rice, which is my favorite food*. This question is on concord. Concord is the agreement between grammatical items. According to the rule of concord, you should use singular verbs for two units that portray a singular idea even though they are combined with *and*. Therefore, *chicken and rice* requires a singular verb.

(102) (C) 2, 4, 3, 1.

The correct order of the paragraph should be as follows: (2) *The atmosphere is grouped into different layers—troposphere, stratosphere, mesosphere, thermosphere and exosphere. (4) The ozone layer is found in the stratosphere, which is 10 km and 80 km from the ground surface, and the greatest concentration is at 25 km from the ground. (3) The depletion of the ozone layer has known and unknown harmful effects. (1) Many countries are trying to control the rate at which the ozone layer is depleting.*

Sentence 2 contains the thesis statement. Sentence 4 should follow sentence 2 because it identifies the subject matter as the ozone layer. Sentence 3 should come after sentence 4 because it supports the problem of the depletion of the ozone layer. Sentence 1 should follow sentence 3 because it tries to proffer a solution to the problem.

(103) (B) 1, 3, 4, 2.

The correct order of the paragraph should be as follows: (1) *A computer is an electronic system, which is used for collecting, storing and producing information. (3) The history of computers can be traced to the creation of automated calculation devices. (4) There are different classifications of computers. (2) Computers should be used cautiously because of their negative aspects.*

Sentence 1 contains the thesis statement and defines *computer*. Sentence 3 should follow sentence 1 because it introduces the beginning era of computers. Sentence 4 should come after sentence 3 because it supports the classification of computers. Sentence 2 should follow sentence 4 because it tries to proffer a solution to the problem.

(104) (D) 3, 1, 2, 4.

The correct order of the paragraph should be as follows: (3) *Drug trafficking is a worldwide unlawful trade that involves the production and distribution of contraband drugs.* (1) *In many nations, the trafficking of drugs is a severe offense that incurs severe penalties.* (2) *Drug trafficking has various debilitating effects on US society.* (4) *Drug trafficking can be eradicated through enlightenment campaigns and stringent policies that prohibit drug abuse.*

Sentence 3 contains the thesis statement and defines *drug trafficking.* Sentence 1 should follow sentence 3 because it broadly highlights the offense of drug trafficking. Sentence 2 should come after sentence 1 because it supports the effect of drug abuse. Sentence 4 should follow sentence 2 because it proffers a solution to the problem of drug trafficking.

(105) (D) 4, 3, 2, 1.

The correct order of the paragraph should be as follows: (4) *Living things are animate creatures, or things that have life.* (3) *Living things are grouped into two main categories: plants and animals.* (2) *Plants can produce their own food, then use it for survival.* (1) *Animals do not have chlorophyll and cannot produce their own food.*

Sentence 4 contains the thesis statement and defines *living things.* Sentence 3 should follow sentence 4 because it gives a broad classification of living things. Sentence 2 should come after sentence 3 because it discusses the first item, plants, in the thesis statement. Sentence 1 should follow sentence 2 because it discusses the second item, animals, in the thesis statement.

(106) (C) 1, 4, 3, 2.

The correct order of the paragraph should be as follows: (1) *Having a flat tire and no idea how to change it can lead to frustration.* *(4) Use bricks or wedges to chock the wheel.* *(3) Jack the vehicle up.* (2) *Use a screwdriver to take off the wheel cover.*

Sentence 1 contains the thesis statement. Sentence 4 should follow sentence 1 because it is the first thing to do when changing a flat tire. Sentence 3 should come after sentence 4 because it is the second thing to do when changing a flat tire. Sentence 2 should follow sentence 3 because it is the third thing to do when changing a flat tire.

(107) (C) Sentence 3.

"*For instance, car owners take the burden of what the emissions cost*" should be inserted after sentence 3, "*Government also intervenes because of external factors, which exist when there is a difference between private costs and social costs.*"

(108) (B) Its.

The **incorrect** sentence reads as follows: *The federal government also intervenes in the public market through the distribution of wealth among <u>our</u> countrymen for sociocultural or political reasons.*

The alternative that will most suitably replace the incorrect underlined <u>our</u> is Option B. *Its* is a singular and possessive pronoun that modifies *federal government*, a singular noun. Option A is not correct because *it's* means *it is*. Option C is wrong because it is a personal possessive pronoun, which shouldn't have a lexical item after it. Option D is wrong because *their* is meant to modify plural items, but *the federal government* is singular.

(109) (C) I.

The correct sentence should read: *The man and I traveled yesterday.* The personal pronoun *I* is used in the subjective case. That is, it is used as the subject of a sentence. It appears before the verb *traveled*. When the first subject, *The man*, is removed from the sentence, we are left with *I*. The sentence now becomes *I traveled yesterday*. Subject pronouns do not come after verbs unless the sentence is an interrogative sentence, or question. Subject pronouns are pronouns used as subjects.

(110) (C) Your.

The correct sentence should read: *Your house is being built.*

This question falls under possessive pronouns. It does not need to take the suffix *-s* because it has a noun after it. It is wrong to say *Yours house is being built.*

(111) (D) Her.

The correct sentence should read: *She saw her on her way to church.*

Her is an object pronoun. It is expected to appear after transitive verbs. The transitive verb in the question is *saw*. The action is performed by the subject *She* and the object *her* receives the action. Examples of object pronouns include *her, us, them, me, him*. A subject pronoun cannot appear after a transitive verb, but it is possible for a subject pronoun to appear after a copular or intensive verb. It is correct to say, *I am he, I am she.* But it is wrong to say, *I am him.*

(112) (B) On.

The correct sentence should read: *He is lying on the bench.*

This question is on preposition usage. *On* is used for things that have surfaces. Examples include beaches, tables, couches and chairs. It is appropriate to say, *I am sitting on the bench. I am lying on the bench. We are on the mountain.* It is the opposite of *in,* which means the inner part of something. For example, *He is in the class.*

(113) (B) With.

The correct sentence should read: *They looked at me <u>with</u> anger.*

This question is on the use of prepositions. *With* is used to describe the manner in which something is done. *With* can also be used to identify an item that was used to perform an action.

(114) (C) A noun.

Anything that has a name is a noun. This could be the names of persons, things, places, animals and others. Examples are *chair, table, Peter, John, dog, chicken, bag, food.* However, in English, usage matters. This means that it is possible for a noun to be used as a verb. For instance, *The cheat is coming.* The word *cheat* is used as a noun. But one can also say, *He will cheat on the exam tomorrow.* In that example, *cheat* is used as a verb.

(115) (B) Sheep.

The correct sentence should read: *I have many <u>sheep.</u>*

The word *sheep* does not take the suffix *-s, -es,* or *-ies.* It is an example of a zero-plural. Such words are followed by singular verbs or plural verbs. To identify whether they are singular or plural, note the presence of a singular or plural verb. For example, *The sheep are dead.* This means there are many sheep (plural). One can also say, *A sheep is missing.* This means the sheep is singular.

(116) (B) Is.

The correct sentence should read: *A pair of glasses is missing.*

When items that come in pairs are used as subjects of a sentence, they can be followed by either singular verbs or plural verbs. When *a pair of* comes before the noun, it is followed by a singular verb. Example: *A pair of shoes is missing.* However, when there is no *A pair of*, a plural verb should be used. Example: *The shoes are missing.*

(117) (A) Are.

The correct sentence should read: *The women, as well as the man, are visiting.*

This is a concord rule in the English language. It is known as subject subordinated concord. It states that when two subjects are joined using *together with*, *alongside*, *along with*, or *as well as*, the first subject determines the verb to be used (whether singular or plural).

(118) (C) Is.

The correct sentence should read: *Mathematics is my favorite subject.*

Mathematics is the subject of the sentence. Grammatical concord says that a singular subject should be followed by a singular verb. *Mathematics* takes the form of plural suffix -*s*, but it is singular. Therefore, *mathematics* is singular and the verb *is* is also singular.

(119) (B) Have.

The correct sentence should read: *A number of students have arrived.*

When *a number of* comes before a noun, it is followed by a plural noun and the verb should be a plural verb. However, if it is *the number of*, it is followed by a plural noun but a singular verb. Example: *A number of people have agreed to the suggestion*. To erase doubts, simply remove *a number of*. Then only *students* is remaining. It becomes *students have arrived*.

(120) (B) Has.

The correct sentence should read: *One-quarter of the building has been completed*.

The noun *building* is in the singular form. It should be followed by a singular verb. But when it is plural, it should be followed by a plural verb. For instance: *Two-quarters of the building has been completed*. The reason for the verb also being singular is the noun coming before it. However, when it is *two-quarters of the buildings*, it should be followed by a plural verb.

(121) (C) Is.

The correct sentence should read: *Twenty thousand dollars is much*.

This is concord of amount. It states that when an amount is used as the subject of a sentence, it should be followed by a singular verb. It's wrong to say, *Twenty thousand dollars are much*. In other words, the amount is considered as singular. Another example is, *Ten kilometers is not far*.

(122) (B) Know.

The correct sentence should read: *Neither Bryan nor the men know her whereabouts*.

This falls under proximity concord. It states that when two subjects are joined using *neither, nor* or *either, or*, the noun closest to the verb determines whether the verb will be singular or plural. The closest noun to the verb is *men*, and *men* is a plural noun. Therefore, it should be followed by a plural verb.

(123) (A) It's.

The correct sentence should read: _It's high time we left this place._

This question is on pronouns and contractions. Pronouns are used in place of nouns. They are used to avoid repetition of nouns in a statement. _It's_ is a contracted form of _It is_. _It's_ is different from _its_ because the latter is a possessive pronoun, which shows ownership and should take a proceeding and modified noun.

(124) (C) Taller.

The comparative form usually ends in _-er_ or _-ier_. It is the form that appears after the positive form. In making a comparison between two items, the comparative form should be used. For instance, _Between Bryan and Cole, who is taller?_ If the comparison is done among three or more items, the superlative form should be used. Other examples of comparative adjectives include _dirtier, bolder, smarter, uglier, luckier._

(125) (B) Adjectives.

Adjectives qualify or describe nouns, pronouns and nominals. Adjectives can be predicative or attributive. In other words, adjectives can appear before nouns or after nouns. Examples of adjectives include _kind, gentle, ugly, peaceful, joyful, slow._

(126) (C) Noun clause.

A noun clause has a noun or pronoun as its key word. It is not a part of speech.

(127) (B) Are.

The correct sentence should read: *My glasses are missing.*

Anything that has two parts (summation plurals) is followed by a plural verb. Examples are *trousers, glasses, scissors, binoculars, pliers, shears*, etc. However, if *a pair of* appears before it, a singular verb is to be used. For example: *A pair of scissors is missing. A pair of trousers was stolen.*

(128) (C) The students were happy.

To be on cloud nine means to be happy. It is an idiomatic expression.

(129) (B) He is in a hard situation.

To have one's back against the wall means to be in a hard situation. This is an idiomatic expression.

(130) (A) Bryan loves Mary.

To be head over heels means to love a person. This is an idiomatic expression.

(131) (B) The wife made his plans fail.

To upset the applecart is another idiomatic expression. It means to make someone's plans fail.

(132) (B) She was not happy.

To be up in arms means to be unhappy or sad. This is another idiomatic expression.

(133) (A) The woman had to please her husband.

To bend over backward is an idiomatic expression that means to please a person even though one is uncomfortable with it.

(134) (A) The workers expressed their feelings.

To make no bones about something is an idiomatic expression meaning to unequivocally express one's feelings about something.

(135) (A) The doctor achieved something last year.

To break new ground is an idiomatic expression meaning to achieve something nobody has achieved before.

(136) (B) The lecturer likes making contradictory statements.

This idiomatic expression is used when people contradict themselves.

(137) (C) Peter works hard.

To burn the candle at both ends is an idiom meaning to be hardworking.

(138) (B) He was trying to make up for lost time.

Working against the clock is an idiomatic expression. It means to be quick or fast in what one is doing as a result of time being wasted.

(139) (A) Humans love pleasure.

The addition of a story will keep the listener interested in the communication. For instance, in a classroom, it is important for the teacher to be able to use a story or two to hold the students' attention. When making a presentation as a Foreign Service officer, remember to add stories for purposes of audience engagement.

(140) (A) Marketplace.

The marketplace is a noisy place. Exclusive information is better shared in a quiet place.

(141) (D) Happiness.

Nonverbal communication is a means of communication without overt speech. Happiness is not a negative nonverbal communication. Negative nonverbal communication does not involve speech. Instead, it involves the use of facial expressions to communicate or convey feelings. Slouching, frowning and silence are all negative nonverbal communications.

(142) (B) It is unappealing to the ear.

While speaking, it is appropriate to speak loudly. If you do not speak loudly, the listener will find it difficult to hear or even understand the message. When the listener does not understand the speaker, communication does not take place. Communication goes two ways.

(143) (D) Procrastinating.

Effective speakers do not procrastinate. Effective speakers are confident, have passion and are direct.

(144) (D) It helps you hear better.

It is necessary to take a deep breath before continuing to speak because it helps you stay steady, gain balance and lets you take a glimpse at your notes. Helping you hear better is not a reason for taking a deep breath before continuing. You take a deep breath to gain more energy.

(145) (A) An audience often does not have a long attention span.

The audience is easily distracted by other things or activities. To keep them interested, the speaker has to be concise.

(146) (B) To give the listener the opportunity to attend to other issues or activities.

Taking a pause during communication does not give the listener the opportunity to attend to other issues or activities. Instead, it enables your words to be compelling, gives the listener an opportunity to pay attention to what is coming next, and it gives the listener some time to think about what you just said.

(147) (A) To show you are conceited.

Learn to establish eye contact with your audience. It shows that you are confident and truthful in the words you speak. Being conceited is not a reason for making eye contact.

(148) (D) Using vague vocabulary.

Using vague vocabulary will have a negative effect on the audience because they will not be able to decipher the message that is being shared.

(149) (D) Shyness.

Confidence is a very important quality when it comes to effective speaking. Confidence makes people see you as an expert and causes them to pay attention to what you are saying. Shyness is not a quality of an effective speaker.

(150) (A) Eager to hear more.

To be a Foreign Service officer who communicates with people effectively, you have to understand and implement some essential communication tools. When you are speaking effectively, your audience wants to hear more. You will need to connect with your audience through storytelling, entertainment, word choice and the content of your speech.

(151) (A) Distort the flow of communication.

An environment filled with noise and disorderliness will distort the flow of communication.

(152) (B) Send a negative message to your audience.

Be conscious of your body language when speaking. Your facial expressions matter. Frowning or raising your brow may send a negative message to your audience. Every society has body language that is considered taboo. You should know some of these movements in order to avoid misunderstandings between you and your audience. Watch out for expressions that show negativity.

(153) (B) Concise.

Effective speakers are known to be concise. They get straight to the point and avoid redundancy. Audiences do not often have a long attention span, and listeners' minds may wander. Effective speakers know where to begin their presentation and when to stop. They quickly get the audience's rapt attention.

Test 1: Essay Answer

College Athletes Deserve to Be Paid

As sporting activities begin to gain momentum in colleges and the NCAA continues to record a considerable amount of income, people are beginning to discuss the idea of paying college athletes.

This could work if we consider several possibilities. For instance, we could leverage a free market approach in which athletes earn what the market can afford or pay at a given point in time. College athletes could make money from signing autographs or acquiring endorsements just like top Olympians do. The organization can also establish a particular amount of money each athlete is allowed to earn.

Those who support the argument above believe that college athletes are the ones doing the work. They train, participate in games and bring in audiences. Thus, they should be compensated. Moreover, there would be no NCAA without the athletes, and the college coaches who receive fat salaries would not get paid. A corporation like Nike would also not profit from each sport. The NCAA generates about $1 billion in revenue annually. However, college athletes do not benefit from this revenue. The proponents of this argument believe that paying college athletes will make them stay in college and not go professional quickly, especially when they sign a contract to remain at the university based on an agreed salary.

Supporters of this argument cite the example of Zion Williamson, a Duke basketball superstar who sustained a knee injury as a freshman. Even if Williamson had not loved playing for Duke, the risk of sustaining another injury or terminating his career before it commenced was not worth it since he was not getting paid. Williamson later declared his interest in the NCAA draft the same year. Paying him would make him stay at Duke, while not paying him would make him weigh his options. About one-third of student-athletes stated that they would remain as collegiate athletes if they were on salary.

What's more, paying athletes would also curb the recruitment scandals that bedevil the NCAA. A notable example is the University of Louisville, whose men's basketball team was stripped of the championship title when it was discovered that coaches were employing sex workers to lure recruits to join the team. There have been cases of scandals ranging from changes in grades to bribes and free cars. Paying college athletes and making their salaries public would curb all these excesses.

Those who argue against paying athletes believe that such an approach could be a disaster for all college sports. They say that college sports would become a bidding war and that only affluent schools would be able to afford top athletes. However, some argue this is already happening, as the best athletes join the most established sporting programs. They also claim that paying athletes would ruin players' morale and trigger envy and jealousy, since both sides know how much they are being paid.

Besides, paying athletes would mean that just a tiny fraction of players would make enough money. Not all athletic departments generate money. Most of the funds the NCAA receives come from men's basketball and football. That means that only the small number of players who are signed would end up making millions of dollars immediately after school—and always at the expense of other players.

Those against the idea of paying athletes also support their argument by emphasizing that athletes are already well compensated. Each top athlete receives scholarships worth tens of thousands of dollars annually. Such athletes receive free textbooks, housing and food along with free medical care and other perks. They are also coached by professionals and can leverage their time in college to gain the attention of professional recruiters. Other college students are not enjoying all these benefits, so why place the athletes on a salary as well?

Lastly, while the NCAA generates massive revenue every year, it remains a not-for-profit organization. Most of the revenue generated is shared among members of the institutions through grants, scholarships, educational programs, conferences and support for Division II and III teams. Delegating a huge portion of that revenue toward paying athletes would stop some of these programs.

While each side has a strong case, it is evident that the dangers of paying athletes outweigh the advantages. While college athletes invest time and energy in paying for their respective schools, they enjoy scholarships and other exclusive perks. Implementing a salary structure would also hinder the smooth running of programs that sustain college sports. Furthermore, some groups would be enriched at the expense of others.

Test 2: Job Knowledge Questions

(1) The United States is made up of _____ states.

(A) 50

(B) 51

(C) 44

(D) 32

(2) The United States consists of _____ departments.

(A) 5

(B) 15

(C) 3

(D) 24

(3) Which of the following best describes the United States government?

(A) Democratic

(B) Monarchical

(C) Authoritarian

(D) None of the above

(4) Congress is the _____ branch of the United States government.

(A) Legislative

(B) Executive

(C) Judiciary

(D) Presidential

(5) What is the least number of representatives a state can have in Congress?

(A) One

(B) Five

(C) Two

(D) Three

(6) The resident commissioner who does not vote in the House of Representatives is from what district?

(A) Columbia

(B) The Virgin Islands

(C) Guam

(D) Puerto Rico

(7) Which of the following presidents have been impeached?

(A) Andrew Johnson

(B) Bill Clinton

(C) Donald Trump

(D) All of the above

(8) Which of the following is not true about the position of vice president?

(A) The vice president is the highest rank in the federal government.

(B) The vice president is a non-elected Senate member.

(C) The vice president is the president of the Senate.

(D) None of the above.

(9) Who led the Revolutionary War of US independence?

(A) Abraham Lincoln

(B) George Washington

(C) Alexander Hamilton

(D) George Bush

(10) What significant event took place between 1861 and 1865 in American history?

(A) The fight for independence

(B) The attainment of the status of world power

(C) The Civil War

(D) The creation of Washington, DC

(11) The civil rights movement started gaining ground in what era?

(A) 1940s

(B) 1890s

(C) 1960s

(D) 1990s

(12) The United States dropped atomic bombs on Japan in what year?

(A) 1941

(B) 1945

(C) 1947

(D) 1942

(13) What is the cause of the diversity in US society?

(A) Large-scale immigration

(B) Lifestyle peculiarity

(C) Freedom

(D) The richness of the culture

(14) The US Department of Commerce's Bureau of the Census does not recognize which of the following as a race?

(A) American Indian

(B) European American

(C) Asian American

(D) Hispanic American

(15) In _____, New York enacted laws against drunk driving.

(A) 1980

(B) 2005

(C) 2014

(D) 2009

(16) The choice of clothing for most Americans is typically _____.

(A) Formal

(B) Casual

(C) Light

(D) Heavy

(17) The United States is not a part of which of the following organizations?

(A) World Customs Organization (WCO)

(B) World Trade Organization (WTo)

(C) Organization for Security and Co-operation in Europe (OSCE)

(D) Economic Community of West Africa States (ECOWAS)

(18) The United States government is _____.

(A) Always a participant in world politics and negotiations

(B) Sometimes nonpartisan

(C) Always in support of what the G7 agrees on

(D) Intent on serving the interest of the World Trade Organization before anything else

(19) The rate of imported oil in the United States is _____.

(A) Greater than the percentage of oil it produces domestically

(B) Greater than the rate it exports

(C) Less than the percentage of oil it produces domestically

(D) Always dropping

(20) Why did the Ronald Reagan doctrine in 1981 protect Saudi Arabia?

(A) It was looking out for the interests of the US government.

(B) It was in a cold war with Iraq.

(C) Saudi Arabia offered the United States monetary aid.

(D) None of the above.

(21) Which organization is in charge of most of the bilateral economic assistance the United States offers?

(A) WHO

(B) IMF

(C) USAID

(D) WTO

(22) When it comes to international politics, the United States is
_____.

(A) Only concerned with political issues

(B) Seldom concerned with sociocultural issues

(C) Reducing its mediation role

(D) Slowly allowing China to take over

(23) Mutual defense collaboration means that _____.

(A) Countries have autonomy.

(B) Participating nations will defend one another when under attack.

(C) Countries will pay one another for help when under attack.

(D) Defense is restricted to countries' military capacity.

(24) Which of the following is true about United States' foreign policy?

(A) It attempts to export democracy to other countries.

(B) It is passive about the political systems of other countries.

(C) It will overtly try to make other nations democratic.

(D) It will not negotiate deals with socialist nations.

(25) North American settlement started in St. Augustine, Florida, where a
_____ settlement was established in 1565.

(A) Japanese

(B) Spanish

(C) African

(D) Indian

(26) In what year did the British Plymouth Company establish a settlement?

(A) 1567

(B) 1577

(C) 1587

(D) 1597

(27) Where did the Dutch establish a North American colony?

(A) Virginia

(B) Quebec

(C) Texas

(D) New York

(28) What was the estimated population of the inhabitants of North and South America before European contact?

(A) 30 million

(B) 40 million

(C) 50 million

(D) 60 million

(29) Who coined the term *Indian*?

(A) Christopher Columbus

(B) Vasco da Gama

(C) Theodore Roosevelt

(D) Jim Collins

(30) What model of work replaced indentured servitude?

(A) Remote working

(B) Slavery

(C) On-site work

(D) None of the above

(31) Who were the first people to ship slaves to the Americas?

(A) Dutch

(B) British

(C) Portuguese

(D) Asians

(32) How many Africans were shipped to the new world as slaves?

(A) 9.5 million

(B) 10.5 million

(C) 11.5 million

(D) 12.5 million

(33) Which of the following is not an agency of foreign affairs?

(A) The Department of Agriculture

(B) The Department of Commerce

(C) The US Agency for International Development

(D) State Security Service

(34) The director general is picked from _____.

(A) The State Security Service

(B) The Foreign Service

(C) The police department

(D) The naval department

(35) Who was the first female Foreign Service officer?

(A) Sandra Peters

(B) Pauline Wellington

(C) Evelyn Chris

(D) Lucile Atcherson Curtis

(36) To be selected to serve the United States as a Foreign Service officer, you need to pass _____.

(A) An oral test assessment only

(B) A written assessment only

(C) Physical training first

(D) Written and oral assessment

(37) The Board of Examiners of the Foreign Service _____.

(A) Supervises the school of Foreign Service

(B) Counsels the secretary of state on how best to administer the Foreign Service

(C) Created the Rogers Act

(D) Administered Foreign Service examinations

(38) When the Department of State requested it, Congress established _____ categories of employees in 1946.

(A) Three

(B) Five

(C) Six

(D) Nine

(39) _____ are also called generalists.

(A) Major generals

(B) Junior diplomats

(C) Diplomats in residence

(D) Foreign Service officers

(40) Who can be impacted by a Foreign Service official's frequent travel?

(A) The junior ranking officers in the Foreign Service

(B) Saboteurs within the Foreign Service administration

(C) The children of Foreign Service officers

(D) New recruits in the Foreign Service

(41) A computer is an electronic machine that _____.

(A) Copies and pastes data

(B) Accepts and processes data

(C) Is specifically for domestic use

(D) Does not need human input to function

(42) Which of the following is true?

(A) A calculator is an example of a computer.

(B) A smartphone is not an example of a computer.

(C) A ceiling fan is an example of a computer.

(D) Every machine that makes our work easier is a computer.

(43) The tangible parts of a computer are called _____.

(A) Hardware

(B) Software

(C) Operating systems

(D) Information

(44) The _____ help(s) the computer perform mathematical operations.

(A) Arithmetic unit

(B) Logic unit

(C) Arithmetic logic unit

(D) Output devices

(45) The light pen, touchscreen, microphone and trackball are _____.

(A) Software

(B) Control units

(C) Input devices

(D) Output devices

(46) _____ organizes or manages the other parts of a computer.

(A) The control unit

(B) The arithmetic unit

(C) The logic unit

(D) The system organizer

(47) Software is classified into _____ and _____.

(A) System/application software

(B) Input/output software

(C) Tangible/intangible software

(D) Control unit/system unit

(48) Computer software that organizes, analyzes and stores data in tabular form is called _____.

(A) Light pen

(B) Database

(C) Desktop publishing

(D) Spreadsheet

(49) A businessman had $1,500. After paying some expenses, he had $500 left. What proportion of his money did he spend?

(A) 2/7

(B) 5/3

(C) 2/5

(D) 2/3

(50) Convert 0.0976 to a percentage.

(A) 97.6%

(B) 976%

(C) 9.76%

(D) 0.976%

(51) You need $12,000 to pay for college. You take a simple interest loan of 4% annually. How much will you pay at the end of three years?

(A) $300

(B) $360

(C) $720

(D) $3,600

(52) The scores of some Foreign Service officers on the FSOT are 50, 70, 60, 70, 65, 80 and 72. Calculate the arithmetic mean score.

(A) 60

(B) 65.29

(C) 70.34

(D) 457

(53) Which of the following is not a factor of production?

(A) Land

(B) Labor

(C) Capital

(D) Buyers

(54) The initiator of all productive plans is _____.

(A) Land

(B) Labor

(C) Capital

(D) Enterprise

(55) Which of the following is not true about entrepreneurs?

(A) They must avoid all risks.

(B) They organize the factors of production.

(C) They are decision-makers.

(D) They may not be the owners of the business.

(56) A business that is managed and profitable to just one person is
_____.

(A) A sole proprietorship

(B) A partnership

(C) A joint-stock company

(D) A public limited liability company

(57) A company that consists of two to 50 owners who have bought shares in the
company is _____.

(A) A partnership

(B) A sole proprietorship

(C) A private limited company

(D) A public limited company

(58) Goods that have close substitutes will experience _____ demand.

(A) Complementary

(B) Composite

(C) Competitive

(D) Derived

(59) The quantity of goods and services producers are willing to create and make available for consumption at a defined price and given period of time is called _____.

(A) Supply

(B) Demand

(C) Productivity

(D) Economics

(60) An economic system in which the means of production are completely owned by the community, which takes part in the income and the labor involved, is _____.

(A) Capitalism

(B) Privatization

(C) Communism

(D) Public economy

Test 2: Situational Judgment Questions

(61) Why does the Foreign Service have different career tracks?

(A) It makes officers.

(B) It helps to create complexities.

(C) The United States government demands it.

(D) It emphasizes specialization and division of labor.

(62) Which of the following is not ideal in Foreign Service administration?

(A) A situation in which Foreign Service officers know all their direct supervisors

(B) Stifling bureaucratic processes

(C) Clarity of given instructions

(D) Respectable leadership

(63) _____ is an essential quality in the Foreign Service.

(A) Discipline

(B) Slothfulness

(C) Tardiness

(D) Envy

(64) When there is a multiplicity of instructions from different sources, _____.

(A) It often leads to conflicts.

(B) There is clarity.

(C) It will lead to unity in command.

(D) It helps officers liaise with other officers.

(65) Everyone in your department should be pursuing _____ goals.

(A) Diverse

(B) Similar

(C) Personal

(D) Undefined

(66) Foreign Service officers are referred to as _____.

(A) Military personnel

(B) Foreigners

(C) Civil servants

(D) Ad hoc staff

(67) In what way(s) can employees be rewarded?

(A) Financially only

(B) Digitally

(C) Monetarily and non-monetarily

(D) Manually

(68) Foreign Service officers should maintain a _____ stance.

(A) Neutral

(B) Prejudiced

(C) Leftist

(D) Right-wing

(69) _____ is needed for the transfer of information, promotion of officers and specialization in roles.

(A) Curiosity

(B) Scalar chain

(C) Communication

(D) The internet

(70) When there's no orderliness in an organization, _____.

(A) There will be productivity.

(B) There will be unity and understanding.

(C) There will be chaos.

(D) The quality of work will go down.

(71) How should supervisors treat employees?

(A) With disrespect

(B) With equity

(C) With special preferences as the occasion demands

(D) It depends on gender

(72) If there's instability in the workplace, _____.

(A) Employees tend to work better.

(B) There is an increase in productivity.

(C) There will be more resignations.

(D) There will be a sense of security.

(73) When employees take insignificant initiative, _____.

(A) It is not worth recognizing.

(B) They should be encouraged to do more.

(C) They should not be promoted.

(D) All of the above.

(74) As a Foreign Service officer, you should _____.

(A) Stay process-minded

(B) Be results oriented

(C) Be creative

(D) All of the above

(75) To be productive, you will have to _____.

(A) Delegate

(B) Communicate

(C) Collaborate with others

(D) All of the above

(76) There is an unexpected project that needs to be done before the end of the week. How do you meet the deadline?

(A) Tell your supervisor you will not be able to meet it.

(B) Delegate the easiest part of the job to friends and supervise them.

(C) Ask your supervisor to extend the deadline.

(D) Get an expert team that your supervisor approves of and delegate tasks according to the team members' respective areas of specialization.

(77) To motivate people, you should remind them of the _____ of their work.

(A) Benefits

(B) Pain

(C) Cost

(D) Process

(78) Your team just acquired several new members. What should you do?

(A) Keep your distance in order to understand them.

(B) Get familiar with each other.

(C) Help the new team members see the difficulties involved in the job.

(D) Relate to the new team members just like you do with other colleagues.

(79) You are a diplomat in a country that is under the sanction of the United States. What should you do if you start favoring the perspective of the citizens of your host country?

(A) Report yourself to your supervisor and seek advice.

(B) Resign immediately.

(C) Defend your opinion.

(D) Stop acting in alignment with the mission given to you.

(80) The best people to work with are _____.

(A) African Americans

(B) Asian Americans

(C) White Americans and Hispanics

(D) None of the above

(81) You can easily trust _____ because they do not often hide their feelings and thoughts.

(A) Sanguines

(B) Melancholics

(C) Phlegmatics

(D) Cholerics

(82) _____ are goal-driven people who set goals and do all they can to achieve them.

(A) Sanguines

(B) Cholerics

(C) Melancholics

(D) Phlegmatics

(83) Expect fewer words from a _____.

(A) Sanguine

(B) Phlegmatic

(C) Choleric

(D) Melancholic

(84) Which of these scenarios upsets a melancholic?

(A) Overlooking details

(B) Being meticulous

(C) Doing what is right

(D) All of the above

(85) When team members understand themselves, then there will be
_____.

(A) Less productivity

(B) Difficulty in getting jobs done faster

(C) Ease in getting tasks done

(D) Greater achievements

(86) Collaboration _____.

(A) Often leads to delay

(B) Consumes a lot of resources

(C) Makes tasks more difficult to complete

(D) Is the easiest, fastest and most productive way of dealing with challenges

(87) In the workplace there should be _____.

(A) Communication gaps

(B) Compulsion

(C) Respectable leadership

(D) Unidentified authority

(88) How many superiors should an officer report to?

(A) One

(B) Two

(C) Three

(D) Four

Test 2: English Expression Questions

Usage of English: Passage 2

(1) Our modern world is driven by technology. (2)Technological developments have transformed the civilization of the human race and now help us innovatively carry out tasks. (3) Electronic equipment, devices, improved means of transportation have provided us with more comfort.

(4) Technology is also useful when we intend to increase our level of output. (5) We do not have to expend too much time and effort in order to efficiently produce quality results. (6) Life has never been as enjoyable, comfortable or easy as we have it today. (7) The fields of banking, education, transportation and communication have evolved due to the advancement of technology.

(8) Technology is now an aspect of our everyday life. (9) The rich are not the only individuals who have access to technology. (10) Ordinary people can now enjoy the luxury technology provides. (11) Globalization and industrialization have made this mass access to technology possible. (12) You do not have to be extremely wealthy to enjoy the luxury of television, computers, refrigerators and other gadgets that almost every middle-class citizen can now possess.

(13) The ancient world would never have thought it possible to share information at the speed we have today. (14) Technological inventions for correspondence which include cellular phone, the internet, fax machine and email, have made communication better than it used to be. (15) We do not have to wait for years or days before our messages are delivered. (16) Communication is now quick and easier.

(89) Which of the following part of sentence 1 should be changed?

(A) No change.

(B) Driven by technology

(C) Our modern

(D) World is

(90) What item is missing in sentence 3?

(A) A period

(B) A conjunction

(C) A pronoun

(D) A semicolon

(91) What should be changed in the structure of sentences 8 and 9?

(A) No change

(B) Our everyday life: The rich are not the only individuals

(C) Our everyday life; The rich are not the only individuals

(D) Our everyday life—The rich are not the only individuals

(92) What is missing in sentence 14?

(A) A comma

(B) A period

(C) An exclamation mark

(D) A colon

(93) What should replace the underlined word in sentence 16?

(A) Quickly

(B) Prompt

(C) Speed

(D) Faster

Sentence Selection

(94) Choose the sentence that is most suitable for standard written English.

(A) The tall man came to the house in order to see the young girl who was wearing a blue shirt.

(B) The tall man came to the house in order to see the young girl in a blue shirt.

(C) The tall man came to the house to see the young girl in a blue shirt.

(D) The tall man came to the house in order to see the young girl who was putting on a blue shirt.

(95) Choose the sentence that is most suitable for standard written English.

(A) The director general is the reason why we are paying the embassy a visit.

(B) The director general is the reason why we are paying the embassy a visit

(C) The director general is the reason we are paying the embassy a visit.

(D) The director general, is the reason why we are paying the embassy a visit.

(96) Choose the sentence that is most suitable for standard written English.

(A) I saw the man, the woman; and the girl in the school.

(B) I saw the man, the woman and the girl in the school.

(C) I saw: the man, the woman; and the girl in the school.

(D) I saw the man; the woman; and the girl in the school.

Sentence Correction I

For each sentence, choose the underlined word(s) that should be replaced to correct the sentence, or identify if there are no errors.

(97) Julia, a tall, beautiful damsel, is the new beauty queen of New York.

(A) No errors

(B) Julia, a tall, beautiful damsel,

(C) the new

(D) queen of

(98) The Congressmen, in conjunction with the Senate, is having a meeting.

(A) No errors

(B) The Congressmen

(C) with

(D) is

(99) A number of houses in the metropolitan area has been demolished without a written and signed consent from the court of law.

(A) No errors

(B) A number of houses

(C) has been demolished

(D) from the court of law

(100) The commander in chief of the armed forces <u>came</u> to the ceremony very late <u>but</u> left <u>early</u>.

(A) No errors

(B) early

(C) came

(D) but

(101) <u>It is recorded</u> that measles <u>were</u> once prevalent in <u>some</u> African nations.

(A) No errors

(B) some

(C) were

(D) It is recorded

Paragraph Organization

(102) Choose the clearest and most organized sentence arrangement.

Sentence 1: Inflation is the increase in the cost of goods and services in a nation's economy at a specific time.

Sentence 2: Inflation can result in protests and revolutions in a nation.

Sentence 3: Tactical economic policies will resolve the problem of inflation.

Sentence 4: The effects of inflation on a nation's economy can be positive or negative.

(A) 1, 2, 3, 4

(B) 1, 4, 2, 3

(C) 3, 2 , 1, 4

(D) 2, 1, 3, 4

(103) Choose the clearest and most organized sentence arrangement.

Sentence 1: There are different ways to prevent the flooding of an area.

Sentence 2: During the rainy season, rivers may stretch beyond their banks.

Sentence 3: Flooding is a great downpour that covers dry land over a certain period of time.

Sentence 4: There are different causes of flooding.

(A) 1, 2, 3, 4

(B) 2, 3, 1, 4

(C) 3, 4, 2, 1

(D) 4, 2, 3, 1

(104) Choose the clearest and most organized sentence arrangement.

Sentence 1: There have been many achievements in space exploration.

Sentence 2: Space exploration is the use of manned or unmanned spacecraft to travel through the universe for the purpose of gathering useful information for humanity.

Sentence 3: Between July 1969 and December 1972, 12 American astronauts went on six different missions to reach the moon.

Sentence 4: The latest invention in space travel is the launching of robotic spacecraft to different planets.

(A) 1, 2, 3, 4

(B) 1, 4, 3, 2

(C) 2, 1, 4, 3

(D) 2, 1, 3, 4

(105) Choose the clearest and most organized sentence arrangement.

Sentence 1: An automobile, also called a car, is a wheeled vehicle used for moving people and goods.

Sentence 2: The word *automobile* is derived from the Greek word *autos,* which means "self," and the Latin word *mobilis,* which means "movable."

Sentence 3: How does a car function?

Sentence 4: Another name for automobile, *car,* is derived from the Latin word *carrus,* which means "wheeled vehicle," or from the Middle English word *carre,* which means "cart."

(A) 1, 2, 3, 4

(B) 1, 2, 4, 3

(C) 2, 1, 3, 4

(D) 2, 1, 4, 3

(106) Choose the clearest and most organized sentence arrangement.

Sentence 1: If you notice smoke or fire around you, contact the fire department and give them your name and address.

Sentence 2: If the fire department asks you to leave the room you are in, do so with caution.

Sentence 3: Fire safety consists of the precautionary procedures involved in preventing or reducing fire outbreaks, which may lead to death, injury or loss of property.

Sentence 4: Some fire hazards are overloaded electrical systems, candles, smoking and ignition sources.

(A) 1, 2, 3, 4

(B) 3, 4, 1, 2

(C) 3, 1, 2, 4

(D) 4, 3, 1, 2

Paragraph Revision

Read these sentences and then answer the questions that follow.

Sentence 1: Students often <u>imagines</u> that public examination bodies are against them.

Sentence 2: The task of creating examination questions often starts a very long time before students take the test.

Sentence 3: The next stage is taking the examination.

Sentence 4: The final process is the meticulous collation of results.

(107) This sentence has been omitted from the list above: *The next process is the registration of students.* The insertion of this sentence would be most suitable after which sentence?

(A) Sentence 1

(B) Sentence 2

(C) Sentence 3

(D) Sentence 4

(108) What word will most suitably replace the underlined item in sentence 1?

(A) Thinking

(B) Imagining

(C) Imagine

(D) Thinks

Choose the correct answer

(109) The word *table* is an example of what type of noun?

(A) Common noun

(B) Abstract noun

(C) Proper noun

(D) Uncountable noun

(110) Which of the following is an uncountable noun?

(A) Chair

(B) Information

(C) Bag

(D) Church

(111) Which of the following is an adverb?

(A) Singing

(B) Wise

(C) And

(D) Frankly

(112) Which of the following is a definite article?

(A) A

(B) The

(C) An

(D) And

(113) Rice and stew _____ my favorite food.

(A) Are

(B) We're

(C) Have

(D) Is

(114) Bread and butter _____ enjoyable.

(A) Is

(B) Are

(C) Were

(D) Will

(115) *A Tale of Two Cities* _____ an interesting book.

(A) Were

(B) Is

(C) Are

(D) Had

(116) Three-quarters of the buildings _____ been destroyed.

(A) Has

(B) Are

(C) Is

(D) Have

(117) The number of criminals in police custody _____ fifty.

(A) Is

(B) Were

(C) Are

(D) Have been

(118) The number of dropouts _____high last year.

(A) Was

(B) Were

(C) Have been

(D) Have not been

(119) The cattle _____ grazing.

(A) Was

(B) Is

(C) Are

(D) Wasn't

(120) People _____ in this house.

(A) Live

(B) Lives

(C) Liveded

(D) Live's

(121) The pastor, together with the church members, _____ traveling.

(A) Are

(B) Is

(C) Were

(D) Weren't

(122) The villagers, along with the boy, _____ sick last week.

(A) Was

(B) Is

(C) Were

(D) Isn't

(123) The situation with hydrogen cars is chicken and egg. What does this mean?

(A) Nobody is buying the cars.

(B) Nobody is making the cars.

(C) There are no hydrogen filling stations, so nobody is buying the cars, so nobody is making them.

(D) They are environmentally a great idea.

(124) The politician believes he is under a cloud. What does this mean?

(A) It is about to rain heavily.

(B) He believes he is suspected of doing something wrong.

(C) He believes he is an honest man.

(D) He believes good things will happen soon.

(125) Ojo always has his head in the clouds. What does this mean?

(A) He loves to daydream.

(B) He loves to interfere in people's affairs.

(C) He loves to see the clouds.

(D) He loves to look for trouble.

(126) The businessman is a small cog in a large wheel. What does this mean?

(A) The man has a car with large wheels.

(B) The man likes gossiping.

(C) The man detests his work.

(D) The man is a small part of a big company.

(127) Samson was left in the cold when he asked for directions. What does this mean?

(A) He felt cold.

(B) He was ignored.

(C) He was insulted.

(D) He was sad.

(128) The principal poured cold water on the secretary's plans. What does this mean?

(A) He poured literal cold water on the secretary.

(B) He was angry.

(C) He criticized the secretary's plans.

(D) He liked the secretary's plans.

(129) The killing of the students by the police brought the issue to a head. What does this mean?

(A) The issue resulted in a crisis.

(B) The issue went to the president.

(C) The issue made everyone happy.

(D) The issue made everyone sad.

(130) The manager, as well as his assistant, _____ here last week.

(A) Was

(B) Were

(C) Is

(D) Are

(131) Which of the following is an abstract noun?

(A) Boy

(B) Bag

(C) Newspaper

(D) Anger

(132) Which of the following can take the suffix -s to show plurality?

(A) Girl

(B) Man

(C) Furniture

(D) Advice

(133) Which of the following can take the suffix -es to show plurality?

(A) Boy

(B) Church

(C) Rat

(D) Room

(134) Which of the following nouns is an example of a mutation plural?

(A) Furniture

(B) Tooth

(C) Church

(D) Brother

(135) Which of these nouns always takes a singular verb?

(A) Furniture

(B) Church

(C) Club

(D) Phone

(136) Which of the following is an example of a summation plural?

(A) Brother

(B) Trousers

(C) Toothbrush

(D) School

(137) Another name for a mass noun is a/an _____.

(A) Countable noun

(B) Uncountable noun

(C) Concrete noun

(D) Common noun

(138) Which of the following is an example of a mass noun?

(A) Water

(B) Pen

(C) Shirt

(D) Bus

(139) Speakers are expected to be _____.

(A) Ambivalent about the information they are imparting

(B) Disinterested in the information they are imparting

(C) Interested in the information they are imparting

(D) Indifferent about the information they are imparting

(140) The speaker should always _____.

(A) Argue with the audience

(B) Understand the audience and their characteristics

(C) Be loud

(D) Engage in unhealthy competition with the audience

(141) How many seconds is enough to establish eye contact?

(A) Two to four

(B) Four to seven

(C) One to six

(D) Six to nine

(142) The speaker should establish eye contact with everybody so that_____.

(A) No person will feel ignored

(B) The audience will know the speaker is serious

(C) The audience will understand the topic better

(D) The speaker will know the number of people in the audience

(143) A diplomat attends to conflicts using all of the following except _____.

(A) The power of words

(B) Composure

(C) Sound judgment

(D) Coercion

(144) It takes _____ and _____ to communicate effectively in crisis situations.

(A) Force/coercion

(B) Wisdom/brutality

(C) Wisdom/partial judgment

(D) Wisdom/knowledge

(145) Hasty judgments often end up being _____.

(A) Correct

(B) Erroneous

(C) Objective

(D) Proper

(146) All except which of the following are expected of every diplomat when conflict arises?

(A) Avoiding taking sides

(B) Using a calm voice

(C) Listening to what both parties have to say

(D) Igniting more conflict between parties

(147) Effective communication is a/an _____ skill.

(A) Unimportant

(B) Essential

(C) Optional

(D) None of the above

(148) Effective communication is for _____.

(A) Politicians and business owners

(B) Traders and farmers

(C) Lawyers and Foreign Service officers

(D) All of the above

(149) _____ do not need effective communication skills.

(A) Tailors

(B) Newscasters

(C) Computer geeks

(D) None of the above

(150) Which of the following is not true about effective speaking?

(A) It is very easy when starting out.

(B) It is void of intrigue.

(C) It is straightforward.

(D) All of the above.

(151) Which of the following is true about effective speaking?

(A) It is not necessary for introverts.

(B) It is complex.

(C) It is straightforward.

(D) It is not necessary in crisis situations.

(152) Effective communication involves which of the following?

(A) Storytelling

(B) The right choice of words

(C) Nonverbal communication

(D) All of the above

(153) _____ makes people see you as an expert so they tune into what you are saying.

(A) Expertise

(B) Listening

(C) Confidence

(D) Honesty

Test 2: Essay Question

There is an argument on the best methodology for approaching the problem of malaria, especially in Sub-Saharan Africa. Some believe that better medication should be administered, while others believe that prevention is the best methodology. What is your opinion on this matter?

Test 2: Job Knowledge Answers and Explanations

(1) (A) 50.

The United States is made of 50 states, 14 independent territories and islands, one federal district and 15 departments.

(2) (B) 15.

The United States is made up of 50 states, 14 independent territories and islands, one federal district and 15 departments. The federal government of the United States is a republic. A republic allows the people to exercise power individually or through representatives. The three branches of the US government are the legislature, the executive and the judiciary.

(3) (A) Democratic.

The US government is neither authoritarian nor monarchical. It practices a democratic system of government.

(4) (A) Legislative.

The legislative branch of the United States is also known as the US Congress. It has the responsibility of creating laws that are approved by the president. The federal Congress is bicameral. It is made of the House of Representatives and the Senate.

(5) (A) One.

The House of Representatives is made of 435 seats, and each one represents a district in the United States. The proportion of representatives per state is based on the state's population. The least number of representatives a state can have is one. The representatives serve two years per term.

(6) (D) Puerto Rico.

Aside from the 435 members who are eligible for voting, there are also six members who do not vote. These additional members are five delegates and one resident commissioner. These delegates are from the following districts: American Samoa, The District of Columbia, the Virgin Islands, the Commonwealth of the Northern Mariana Islands and Guam. The resident commissioner who does not vote is from Puerto Rico.

(7) (D) All of the above.

Only three presidents have gone through impeachment procedures. They are Andrew Johnson, Bill Clinton and Donald Trump, whom the House of Representatives impeached twice. The Senate did not vote to impeach any of these three presidents.

(8) (A) The vice president is the highest rank in the federal government.

After the president, the next highest rank in the federal government is the vice president. According to Article I, Section III, Clause IV-V, the vice president is the president of the Senate. As ex officio, that is a non-elected Senate member. The vice president can cast a vote when there is a tie.

(9) (B) George Washington.

General George Washington was the leader of the Revolutionary War, which led to independence. In Philadelphia in 1776, there was a Continental Congress, which proclaimed the independence of the United States. In 1783, participants signed a peace treaty that identified the borders of the nascent nation. George Washington and Alexander Hamilton were the first president and chief advisor of the nation, respectively.

(10) (C) The Civil War.

When the Confederacy attacked a federal property in 1861, the Civil War began. The war ended when the US government defeated the Confederacy in 1865. Slavery was finally abolished on December 6, 1865, by the Thirteenth Amendment. This led to a Reconstruction era, during which voting and legal rights were given to freed slaves.

(11) (C) 1960s.

During the 1960s, the civil rights movement had gained so much ground that there was a social reformation of voting and other forms of sociopolitical discrimination. African Americans and other minority racial groups' rights to vote were recognized in the Constitution.

(12) (B) 1945.

In 1941, when Japan bombed Pearl Harbor, the United States declared war on Japan and joined the Allied nations in conquering fascist Italy and Nazi Germany. In 1945, the United States dropped atomic bombs on two cities in Japan, Hiroshima and Nagasaki, ending the war in the Pacific.

(13) (A) Large-scale immigration.

The United States has a diversity of ethnicity and race. This is due to large-scale immigration throughout its history. US society is a western culture that has unique music, dialects, food, games, lifestyle, and literature. The values of the

United States are secular, rational, and self-expressive. It takes after the British culture, which established itself in North America during the colonial era.

(14) (D) Hispanic American.

The races that the US Department of Commerce's Bureau of the Census recognizes are Native Americans, which are also known as American Indian; White, which is European American; Asian American and African American. Some people argue that Hispanic Americans are a racial group, but the US government categorizes Hispanics as an ethnic group.

(15) (A) 1980.

In 1980, New York enacted tight laws against drunk driving. This measure contrasts with the early years of US society. In the early nineteenth century, alcohol was not prohibited in any way in the United States. It was always available. However, restrictions started cropping up during the temperance movement as the nineteenth century came to an end.

(16) (B) Casual.

Americans' choice of clothing is predominantly informal. Formal wear is mostly used for professional occasions. Cultural roots also have an effect on individuals' style of dress.

(17) (D) Economic Community of West African States (ECOWAS).

The United States participates economically and as a member in the following organizations: World Customs Organization; World Trade Organization;

Organization for Security and Co-operation in Europe (OSCE); Organization of American States; Group of Seven (G7); USMCA, the regional trade bloc with Canada and Mexico; Asia-Pacific Economic Cooperation (APEC) and Organisation for Economic Co-operation and Development (OECD).

(18) (B) Sometimes nonpartisan.

The United States government is sometimes nonpartisan. It is not in the foreign policy of the United States to compulsorily participate in all agreements that the international community agrees to and abides by. It does not matter whether other advanced countries are in agreement. If it does not suit the interests of the United States, then the United States is not obligated to support such agreements.

(19) (A) Greater than the percentage of oil it produces domestically.

A 2014 report shows that the United States produces approximately 66% of the oil that it uses. Since the 1990s, the importation rate of petroleum has always been more significant than the percentage of oil the country produces domestically.

(20) (A) It was looking out for the interests of the US government.

The president after Carter, Ronald Reagan, continued with the doctrine in 1981. His doctrine stated that the United States would offer protection to Saudi Arabia, which was threatened by the Iran and Iraq war. Some analysts conclude that the Carter and Reagan doctrines contributed to the outbreak of the Iraq war in 2003.

(21) (C) USAID.

The US Agency for International Development (USAID) is in charge of most of the bilateral economic assistance the United States offers. However, the Treasury Department takes control of multilateral assistance. In 2014, the $23 billion the United States gave in international donations made it the biggest foreign donor. Also, foreign aid in the United States is political because liberals seem to provide more foreign aid than conservatives.

(22) (C) Reducing its mediation roles.

Currently, there are debates over the necessity and impact of the reductions in the United States' mediation roles. The US military is also concerned about political and sociocultural stability in Afghanistan and Iraq's governments. It is interested in Russian activities in Ukraine and what Saudi Arabia is doing in Yemen. More currently, the 2021 administration of President Joe Biden has declared the end of military interventions in Afghanistan.

(23) (B) Participating nations will defend one another when under attack.

Mutual defense collaboration means that participating nations will defend one another when under attack. The US government has mutual defense agreements with Japan, New Zealand, Australia, the Philippines, South Korea, Thailand and countries that were once in the Southeast Asia Treaty Organization. The United States is also in a mutual defense agreement with South America, the Caribbean and Central America. This agreement is based on the Inter-American Treaty of Reciprocal Assistance.

(24) (A) It attempts to export democracy to other countries.

This is true. There are ongoing studies seeking to identify how successful the United States has been in exporting democracy to other countries. Some people say that American efforts to transfer democracy to other parts of the world have mostly been futile.

(25) (B) Spanish.

North American European settlement began in St. Augustine, Florida, where a Spanish settlement was established in 1565.

(26) (C) 1587.

The British Plymouth Company established its settlement in Roanoke, which is present-day Virginia, in 1587

(27) (D) New York.

In 1609, the Dutch established a colony in what is now known as New York.

(28) (C) 50 million.

An estimated 50 million indigenous people lived in North and South America before Europeans arrived.

(29) (A) Christopher Columbus.

Christopher Columbus coined the term *Indian* because he believed he had arrived in the East Indies, now known as East and Southeast Asia.

(30) (B) Slavery.

Indentured servitude was gradually replaced by slavery as indentured servants gained their freedom.

(31) (C) Portuguese.

Portuguese ships brought African slaves to North America in the 1500s

(32) (D) 12.5 million.

A total of 12.5 million Africans are estimated to have been transported to the New World as slaves.

(33) (D) State Security Service.

This is not an agency of foreign affairs. Workers in the Foreign Service work in the headquarters of any of the four agencies for foreign affairs. These agencies include the Department of State, which has its headquarters in the Harry S Truman building in Washington, DC, the Department of Agriculture, the Department of Commerce and the US Agency for International Development.

(34) (B) The Foreign Service.

Currently, Carol Perez is the director general of the Foreign Service. The position of the director general of the Foreign Service is appointed by the president, with the suggestion and approval of the Senate.

(35) (D) Lucile Atcherson Curtis.

The position of the director general is not gender-selective. As of 2021, the past four directors general of the Foreign Service have been women. The first female Foreign Service officer was Lucile Atcherson Curtis. In 1923, she was appointed as a US diplomatic officer/consular officer, positions that were combined in 1924 as a Foreign Service officer.

(36) (D) Written and oral assessment.

To be selected to serve the United States as a Foreign Service officer, you need to pass different written and oral assessments. Foreign Service officers are assigned to one of the 265 US diplomatic bases all over the world. These diplomatic missions include consulates, embassies and other US facilities.

(37) (D) Administered Foreign Service examinations.

The Rogers Act created the Board of Examiners of the Foreign Service for the administration of Foreign Service examinations. The Rogers Act was also the progenitor of the Board of the Foreign Service, which was to counsel the secretary of state on how best to administer the Foreign Service. The civil servants working in the agricultural and commercial extensions were already diplomats, but they were not Foreign Service officers until the legislation was passed.

(38) (C) Six.

When the Department of State requested it, the US Congress passed a Foreign Service Act in 1946 that established six categories of employees: Foreign Service officers, chiefs of mission, Foreign Service reservists, Foreign Service staff, consular agents and alien personnel who were later called Foreign Service nationals (then changed to locally employed staff).

(39) (D) Foreign Service officers.

Foreign Service officers are also called generalists. They receive an appointment from the president upon the suggestion and approval of the Senate. They specialize in specific subject areas and carry out the primary duties of the Foreign Service. They are selected only after going through oral and written assessments. Foreign Service officers are diplomats meant to carry out a diplomatic function.

(40) (C) The children of Foreign Service officers.

Children are affected by the career path their Foreign Service parent has chosen. They are raised far from their friends, who get to enjoy a continuous upbringing in a society they are familiar with. That said, most Foreign Service officers' children get more international exposure due to the eclectic environment and people they associate with.

(41) (B) Accepts and processes data.

A computer is an electronic machine that accepts and processes data, then produces information. A computer is programmed to automatically work out logical operations. A complete computer system is made up of hardware, software or operating system and peripheral tools. A computer may function as a unit or a network. We can find computerized systems in almost every aspect of our modern world, including both industrial and domestic use.

(42) (A) A calculator is an example of a computer.

This is true. Computerized systems are as basic as remote controls and as complex as special-purpose robots. Your calculator or smartphone are examples of computers. This is because a computer is an electronic machine that accepts and processes data, then gives out information. A computer is programmed to automatically work out logical operations.

(43) (A) Hardware.

Hardware includes all the tangible parts of a computer. This includes a motherboard, circuits, cables, computer chips, graphics cards, keyboards, sound cards, printers, displays and memory (RAM). A computer that serves general use has four main parts: the arithmetic logic unit (ALU), the input and output devices, the memory, and the control unit. These parts are interconnected.

(44) (C) Arithmetic logic unit.

The arithmetic logic unit (ALU) helps the computer perform arithmetic and logical operations. These operations include addition, subtraction, multiplication, division, square roots, sine, etc. It assists in solving complex mathematical problems at a faster speed. It is the calculator of the computer system.

(45) (C) Input devices.

Input devices send data to the computer. The CPU processes the data before it is produced as information through the output device. Examples of input devices are a keyboard, mouse, image scanner, camera, joystick, light pen, touch screen, microphone and trackball. They complement the other main parts of the computer, which are the arithmetic logic unit (ALU), the output devices, the memory and the control unit.

(46) (A) The control unit.

The control unit is also called the control system because it organizes or manages the other parts of a computer. It first reads then interprets the instructions of a program, then it changes them into control signals, which activate other components of the computer system. The combination of the ALU, the control unit and registers collectively forms the central processing unit (CPU).

(47) (A) System/application software.

Software is classified into system and application software. System software includes Unix, BSD, Linux, DOS, Mackintosh operating system and Microsoft

Windows. Application software includes database management, desktop publishing, spreadsheets, internet access, graphics, audio and games. The software is the intangible component of the computer. They are immaterial. Examples are protocols, programs, data, etc. The software includes computer-encoded instructions or information.

(48) (D) Spreadsheet.

A spreadsheet is computer software that organizes, analyzes and stores data in tabular form. Spreadsheets were invented to make paper worksheets computerized or digital. The spreadsheet application works on the data that has been inputted into the tabular cells. The cells take in numerical and alphabetical data and signs, then automatically operate on them to produce results. Its value is based on the data entered into the cells.

(49) (D) 2/3.

Since the whole is $1,500 and he had just $500 left, the proportion of money he spent was:

$1,500/1500 - $500/1,500

= $1,000/1,500

Divide the numerator and denominator by 500, which is the highest common factor.

$1,000 divided by 500 = $2

$1,500 divided by 500 = $3

Only 2/3 would be left.

(50) (A) 97.6%.

To make it easier, convert 0.0976 to a fraction. That is:

0.0976 = 976/1,000

Now, multiply this value by 100.

976/1,000 × 100

You can divide 100 by 100 and 1,000 by 100. The result will be 976/10.

Further division of this will be 97.6%.

(51) (D) $3,600.

Here's the formula for solving simple interest:

Simple interest = P × r × n

P is $3,000

r is 4%

n is 3

Therefore:

= $3,000 × 4/100 × 3

= $360

The sum that would be paid is:

Interest + principal loan

= $3,000 + $360

= $3,360.

(52) (B) 65.29.

First, add up the figures in any order because it will not affect the value of the total score.

$50 + 70 + 60 + 70 + 65 + 80 + 72 = 457$

Divide 457 by the total number of figures, which is 7.

Therefore, $457 \div 7 = 65.29$.

(53) (D) Buyers.
This is not a factor of production. The factors of production are land, labor, capital and enterprise. Production is the creation of utility or goods and services and the satisfaction of desires or wants, which are remunerated in the form of payment. It is the utility of specific factors, which are also known as factors of production, for the creation of these goods and services.

(54) (B) Labor.

Some economists prefer to call labor the prime mover because it is the initiator of all productive plans. Without labor, all other processes of production will become fallow. Labor refers to all kinds of effort exerted toward the utility of available resources for production. Labor can be mental, manual, skilled or unskilled. Labor is often rewarded after the completion of a task.

(55) (A) They must avoid all risks.

This is not true. Entrepreneurs are in charge of controlling and organizing all the factors of production for the purpose of production. They may be directors, managers or owners of a public or private enterprise. They bear the risks involved in the production and distribution of goods and services.

(56) (A) A sole proprietorship.

This is a business that is managed by just one person. That person may receive assistance from family members. A sole proprietorship business is often very easy to organize, and the owner can make decisions without the obstacles of bureaucratic processes. A sole proprietorship business does not have limited liability.

(57) (C) A private limited company.

A private limited company consists of two to 50 owners who have bought shares in the company. The shares are not open for sale to the public, and a shareholder cannot sell shares without the consent of other shareholders. This sort of business also offers the advantage of limited liability. When there is a need for the liquidation of the company, it does not affect the shareholders' personal assets.

(58) (C) Competitive.

There are five general classifications of demand—competitive demand, derived demand, complementary or joint demand, composite demand and independent demand. In competitive demand, some goods and services have close substitutes. This means that there are other competitors who have similar goods and services. An example is the cell phone industry. When the price of any of these commodities increases, the substitute product may also see an increase in demand from consumers.

(59) (A) Supply.

Supply is the quantity of goods and services producers are willing to create and make available for consumption at a defined price and period of time. Supply is not always stable. It is affected by factors such as the price of the goods and services, the price of complementary and competing goods and services, income, population size, changes in preferences of consumers, environmental and social conditions and government policies.

(60) (C) Communism.

Communism is the culmination of socialism. It is idealistic in principle. Like socialism, all the means of production are owned by the community, which takes part in the income and the labor involved. Communism is theoretically a process that goes through four stages of social evolution—bourgeois capitalism, dictatorship of the proletariat, which becomes socialism, and then communism.

Test 2: Situational Judgment Answers and Explanations

(61) (D) It emphasizes specialization and division of labor.

The Foreign Service has different career tracks because it emphasizes specialization and division of labor. When there is an appropriate division of work, there is efficiency, speed and order. The number one rule in management is delegation. Tasks should be delegated to the best hands. The rule of specialization should be applied so that everyone gets to do what they are passionate about and skilled at.

(62) (B) Stifling bureaucratic processes.

Bureaucracy should not create vast communication or association gaps between the authorities/managing body and the employees. As a Foreign Service officer, you must always know who you directly report to and be sure there is no ambiguity in given instructions. There should be room for questioning for the purpose of clarity and redress on complex issues.

(63) (A) Discipline.

Discipline is an essential quality in the Foreign Service. When there is no discipline, there will be no productivity. Discipline ensures that everyone does their job without unnecessary coercing or overbearing supervision.

(64) (A) It often leads to conflicts.

Every employee or Foreign Service officer should report to just one boss. A multiplicity of instructions from different bosses often results in confusion and conflict. This is called disunity in command. Therefore, authorities should not interfere with the affairs of employees who are not directly below them.

(65) (B) Similar.

Everyone in your department should be pursuing the same or similar goals. This is called unity of direction. The goals must be specific, measurable, attainable, relevant to making an impact on the US economy and time bound. That is why you should be aware of the decade, yearly, quarterly, monthly, weekly and daily goals of the current US administration and your department.

(66) (C) Civil servants.

Foreign Service officers are referred to as civil servants because they are in the field to serve the United States. It is wrong and unconstitutional to put your personal interests above your nation. Even if the situation conflicts with the goals of your nation of origin, you must forgo personal sentiments and work toward US goals.

(67) (C) Monetarily and non-monetarily.

Rewards are factors that should be considered in management. Rewards can be either financial or non-financial. They can be praise, recognition, a day off, etc.

(68) (A) Neutral.

Henri Fayol believed that management should maintain a neutral stance. He stated that a balanced approach to power-sharing is the best way to manage an organization.

(69) (B) Scalar chain.

Fayol stipulates that there is a need for a hierarchy that starts from the top and flows to the bottom. Every officer should know and have direct access to their superiors. The scalar chain is needed for the transfer of information, promotion of officers and specialization in roles.

(70) (C) There will be chaos.

When there is no orderliness, the new order will be frustration, lack of productivity and chaos.

(71) (B) With equity.

In the workplace, you should treat everyone with equity. There should be no racial, gender, religious, or personal biases. No employee or customer should face discrimination. For example, it is common for some people to categorize all Muslims as terrorists and therefore treat individuals from this background with suspicions and prejudice. Some persons still practice White supremacy. They believe people with White skin color are superior to people from other races.

(72) © There will be more resignations.

Employees tend to work better if there is stability in the workplace. If the administration offers job security, fewer penalties and an enabling environment, employees will feel safe to invest their time and effort. Administrators must give workers an assurance of their investment in labor through pensions, social welfare and less downsizing.

(73) (B) They should be encouraged to do more.

Authorities should encourage initiative. When workers see that their initiative is recognized in the organization, they will do more. No matter how insignificant the initiative may seem, employees should be recognized for their hard work and ideas.

(74) (D) All of the above.

As a Foreign Service officer, you have to take an innovative approach toward problem-solving. Do not be too traditional or conservative in your methodologies. Be open to new ideas. Stay process minded and results oriented.

(75) (D) All of the above.

In the work arena, there should be trust, understanding and loyalty to the mission. Foreign Service officers of the United States must always put their nation first. To be productive, you will have to delegate, communicate and collaborate with other Foreign Service officers who share the same values as you.

(76) (D) Get an expert team that your supervisor approves of and delegate tasks according to the team members' respective areas of specialization.

This question emphasizes the need for teamwork and division of labor. In this kind of scenario, you need your supervisor's approval. Remember that team members must understand themselves so that it will be easy to get tasks done. They must understand the vision and mission and be technically fit for the task.

(77) (A) Benefits.

Motivation is a key factor in the workplace. Foreign Service officers who are motivated through monetary rewards or other forms of reward tend to be more productive. Humans are wired to stake their time and efforts on things that will gratify them personally. Apply this rule when dealing with people as a diplomat. Do not be too quick to make your own interests obvious.

(78) (B) Get familiar with each other.

For effective collaboration, you must consider the other person's emotional state. Humans like to give their time, attention and approval to people who seem to understand them or what they do. Therefore, you should seek to understand the new people you are working with.

(79) (A) Report yourself to your supervisor and seek advice.

This question is meant to weigh your action in a clientitis situation. You need to always remember that America should always come first in your activities. How you feel or think about some issues should not interfere with your loyalty to the United States.

(80) (D) None of the above.

This question is testing you on the aspect of impartiality. As a diplomat, you must be ready to work with everyone without personal prejudices. The duty of a Foreign Service officer demands collaboration and nondiscrimination.

(81) (A) Sanguines.

Sanguine are extroverts. They like to go out. They derive joy in relating with people. They relish teamwork and fellowship. They don't hide their feelings or thoughts.

(82) (B) Cholerics.

Cholerics are goal-driven people who set goals and do all they can to achieve them. They have a positive attitude toward their plans and are not discouraged even when facing obstacles.

(83) (B) Phlegmatics.

Phlegmatics are conservative or quiet. Give them time to think about matters when there is an issue that calls for a decision.

(84) (A) Overlooking details.

Melancholics are often very cautious when making decisions. They are often obsessed with details and can be perfectionists. They tend to operate by the book.

(85) (C) Ease in getting tasks done.

Team members must understand themselves before they can accomplish the tasks set before them.

(86) (D) Is the easiest, fastest and most productive way of dealing with challenges.

As a Foreign Service officer, you should be ready to divide tasks among team members. Collaboration is the easiest, fastest and most productive way of dealing with challenges. When there is an appropriate division of work, there is efficiency, speed and order. The number one rule in management is delegation. Tasks should be delegated to the best hands.

(87) (C) Respectable leadership.

Respectable leadership that influences but does not forcefully compel is what every managing body should use to make workers find their jobs enjoyable.

(88) (A) One.

Every employee or Foreign Service officer should report to just one boss. A multiplicity of instructions from different bosses often results in confusion and conflict. This is called disunity in command. Therefore, authorities should not interfere with employees who are not directly below them.

Test 2: English Expressions Answers and Explanations

(89) (B) Driven by technology.

This sentence is in the passive voice. It is better to write this sentence in the active voice. That is, the subject of the verb should precede the object of the action. So, it becomes, "Technology is driving the world."

(90) (B) A conjunction.

Conjunctions are used to combine phrases and clauses, show contrast or suggest an alternative. Examples are *and, or, but, also*, etc. The conjunction *and* is missing in the given sentence. It should have read, *"Electronic equipment, devices and improved means of transportation..."*

(91) (A) No change.

There are no errors in sentences 8 and 9.

(92) (A) A comma.

Relative pronouns like *who, which, what* and *whose* often take a comma before and after they are used. Whenever a relative pronoun appears after a noun or a pronoun, the noun, pronoun or nominal determines the verb to be used.

(93) (D) Faster.

"Communication is now faster and easier." *Faster* is used to compare two things.

(94) (C) The tall man came to the house to see the young girl in a blue shirt.

This option is more concise than the other options. It briefly presents the message without altering the meaning. It is clear and unambiguous.

(95) (C) The director general is the reason we are paying the embassy a visit.

This option is more concise than the other options. It briefly presents the message without altering the meaning. It is clear and unambiguous.

(96) (B) I saw the man, the woman and the girl in the school.

All the other options are not properly punctuated.

(97) (A) No errors.

The phrase *a tall, beautiful damsel* is in appositive to *Julia*. This means that the phrase is adding more information to *Julia*. It is describing Julia. An appositive is sometimes called a zero-relative clause because it does not contain a relative pronoun (*who, which, that, whose, where, when,* etc.). Therefore, there need to be commas to separate the appositive from the item that is being described.

(98) (D) Is.

The subject in this statement is *the Congressmen*. It is plural. Therefore, the verb should be plural.

(99) (C) Has been demolished.

When the lexical item *number of* is used, and the statement starts with the definite article *the*, the verb should be singular. This shows that the writer is being specific. However, it should be plural if the statement starts with the indefinite articles *a* or *an*. The indefinite article means that the subject is undefined or not specific. Therefore, the verb *have* should have been used in his instance.

(100) (A) No errors.

Conjunctions (*and, or, but, also*, etc.) are used to combine phrases and clauses, show contrast or suggest an alternative. The sentence semantically requires a contrasting conjunction. *And* is used to combine phrases and clauses. *But* is used to show contrast. *Or* is used to suggest an alternative.

(101) (C) Was.

This question is on concord. There are some singular nouns that look like plurals because they take the -*s* form, but they are not plural, and they should be used with singular verbs. *Measles* is one such word. Other examples are *mathematics, linguistics, gymnastics, athletics, Athens, Algiers, news, barracks*, etc.

(102) (B) 1, 4, 2, 3.

The correct paragraph structure is: (1) *Inflation is the increase in the cost of goods and services in a nation's economy at a specific time. (4) The effects of inflation on a nation's economy can be positive or negative. (3) Tactical economic policies will resolve the problem of inflation. (2) Inflation can result in protests and revolutions in a nation.*

Sentence 1 contains the thesis statement and defines *inflation*. Sentence 4 should follow sentence 1 because it generally states the effect of the subject matter, inflation. Sentence 2 should come after sentence 4 because it supports the effect of inflation. Sentence 3 should follow sentence 2 as the final paragraph because it tries to provide a solution to the problem.

(103) (C) 3, 4, 2, 1.

The correct paragraph structure is: *(3) Flooding is a great downpour that covers dry land over a certain period of time. (4) There are different causes of flooding. (2) During the rainy season, rivers may stretch beyond their banks. (1) There are different ways to prevent the flooding of an area.*

Sentence 3 contains the thesis statement and defines *flood*. Sentence 4 should follow sentence 3 because it introduces the causes of flooding. Sentence 2 should come after sentence 4 because it supports the problem of flooding. Sentence 1 should follow sentence 2 as the final paragraph because it tries to provide a solution to the problem of flooding.

(104) (D) 2, 1, 3, 4.

The correct paragraph structure is: *(2) Space exploration is the use of manned or unmanned spacecraft to travel through the universe for the purpose of gathering useful information for humanity. (1) There have been many achievements in space exploration. (3) Between July 1969 and December 1972, 12 American astronauts went on six different missions to reach the moon. (4) The latest invention in space travel is the launching of robotic spacecraft to different planets.*

Sentence 2 contains the thesis statement and defines *space exploration*. Sentence 1 should follow sentence 2 because it broadly highlights the achievements of space exploration. Sentence 3 should come after sentence 1 because it supports the achievements in space exploration. Sentence 4 should follow sentence 3 because it narrows down the inventions in space travel.

(105) (B) 1, 2, 4, 3.

The correct paragraph structure is: *(1) An automobile, also called a car, is a wheeled vehicle used for moving people and goods. (2) The word automobile is derived from the Greek word autos, which means "self," and the Latin word mobilis, which means "movable." (4) Another name for automobile, car, is derived from the Latin word carrus, which means "wheeled vehicle," or from the Middle English word carre, which means "cart." (3) How does a car function?*

Sentence 1 contains the thesis statement and defines *automobile*. Sentence 2 should follow sentence 1 because it gives a narrow definition of the word *automobile*. Sentence 4 should come after sentence 2 because it discusses more about the word *automobile*. Sentence 3 should follow sentence 4 because it discusses the function of the subject matter.

(106) (B) 3, 4, 1, 2.

The correct paragraph structure is: *(3) Fire safety consists of the precautionary procedures involved in preventing or reducing fire outbreaks, which may lead to death, injury or loss of property. (4) Some fire hazards are overloaded electrical systems, candles, smoking and ignition sources. (1) If you notice smoke or fire around you, contact the fire department and give them your name and address. (2) If the fire department asks you to leave the room you are in, do so with caution.*

Sentence 3 contains the thesis statement and defines *fire safety*. Sentence 4 should follow sentence 3 because it tells more about the subject matter, fire. Sentence 1 should come after sentence 4 because it is the first thing to do when there is a fire outbreak. Sentence 2 should follow sentence 1 because it is the next thing to do.

(107) (B) Sentence 2.

The correct option is B because the omitted item, "*The next process is the registration of students,*" is the continuation of sentence 2, "*The task of creating examination questions often starts a very long time before students take the test."*

(108) (C) Imagine.

The **incorrect** sentence is: *Students often <u>imagines</u> that public examination bodies are against them.*

Option C is the correct answer because the subject of the sentence is plural; therefore, the verb should take the plural form, *imagine*, not the singular form *imagines*. Option A is wrong because the subject matter should not take the continuous verb *thinking*. Option B is wrong because the subject matter should not take the continuous verb *imagining*. Option D is wrong because the subject of the sentence is plural; therefore, the verb should be plural.

(109) (A) Common noun.

Table is a common noun. Anything that has a surface with legs that enable it to stand is termed or known as a table. It is a general name. It is not an uncountable noun, an abstract noun or a proper noun. It can also be regarded as a concrete noun because tables can be seen and touched.

(110) (B) Information.

Uncountable nouns are nouns that cannot or should not be counted. Nouns such as *information, baggage, luggage, advice* and *damage* are all uncountable nouns. They are expected to be followed by singular verbs. They do not take the suffixes -*s*, -*es* or *ies*. You can say *some baggage, some information* and *some luggage*. But it is wrong to say *some informations, some baggages* and *some luggages*.

(111) (D) Frankly.

Adverbs modify verbs, adjectives, adverbs and other parts of speech. Adverbs often take the suffixes *-ly*, *-ward* and *-wise*. For example, *I traveled eastward last year*. Just add *-ly* to an adjective to make it an adverb. For instance, *beautiful* becomes *beautifully*. An adverb always tells us more about the action or the description of an adjective.

(112) (B) The.

The definite article *the* is used for something a person is familiar with. It is used to show that the speaker is being specific. *A* and *an* are indefinite articles. They are used when the speaker is not trying to be specific. For example, *The man is here*. This means that the speaker has knowledge of the man. This is quite different from *A man is here*. In this case, the speaker does not have knowledge of the man.

(113) (D) Is.

The correct sentence is: *Rice and stew is my favorite food*.

This question falls under concord, which is the agreement between the subject and the predicate. The two subjects are regarded as one, so a singular verb is to be used. Other examples of singular subjects include *bow and arrow, bread and butter* and *chicken and rice*. These kinds of subjects are often complementary in nature. That is, they work together.

(114) (A) Is.

The correct sentence is: *Bread and butter is enjoyable*.

This question falls under concord, which is the agreement between the subject and the predicate. The two subjects are regarded as one, so a singular verb is to be used.

(115) (B) Is.

The correct sentence is: *A Tale of Two Cities is an interesting book.*

The subject, *A Tale of Two Cities*, is singular. Do not be confused with the presence of the plural noun *cities* before the verb. The subject is still singular and should take a singular verb for the sake of concord.

(116) (D) Have.

The correct sentence is: *Three-quarters of the buildings have been destroyed.*

The rule of concord of percentage states that the noun closest to the verb determines whether it will be a singular verb or a plural verb. The last word before the verb is *buildings*, which is in the plural form. So the verb will also be in the plural form. You can remove *three quarters of* and what is left is *the buildings*. It becomes *The buildings have been destroyed.*

(117) (A) Is.

The correct sentence is: *The number of criminals in police custody is fifty.*

When the lexical item *number of* is used, the verb should be singular if the statement starts with the definite article *the*. However, it should be plural if the statement starts with the indefinite articles *a* or *an*. Here are some examples: *The number of US officials around is fifty. A number of houses have been demolished. A number of parents were here.*

(118) (A) Was.

The correct sentence is: *The number of dropouts <u>was</u> high last year*

When the lexical item *number of* is used, the verb should be singular if the statement starts with the definite article *the*. However, it should be plural if the statement starts with the indefinite articles *a* or *an*.

(119) (C) Are.

The correct sentence is: *The cattle <u>are</u> grazing.*

The word *cattle* is an unmarked plural. These are nouns that resemble or look like singular nouns but are actually plural. As such, plural verbs are used after them. They do not take the *-s* form. They should always be used with plural verbs. Examples are *cattle, clergy, people*.

(120) (A) Live.

The correct sentence is: *People <u>live</u> in this house.*

This question is on concord. The subject *people* is plural and is followed by a plural verb. The verb *live* has four forms: *live, lives, living, lived*. The base form of a verb is the plural form. So, it is proper to say, *They live in the house* rather than *They lives in the house*. The *-s* form of a verb is the singular form.

(121) (B) Is.

The correct sentence is: *The pastor, together with the church members, <u>is</u> traveling.*

Ignore words that look like the coordinator *and* but are not. They are called pseudo coordinators because they look like coordinators. This includes *as well as, in addition to, in the company of, alongside, in conjunction with*, etc. They should not affect the nature of the verb.

(122) (C) Were.

The correct sentence is: *The villagers, along with the boy, were sick last week.*

In this case, the first subject is in the plural form *villagers*. As such, the verb should be in the plural form *were*. *Were* is the past tense of *are*.

(123) (C) There are no hydrogen filling stations, so nobody is buying the cars, so nobody is making them.

A chicken-and egg-situation means being unable to tell or identify the cause of something.

(124) (B) He believes he is suspected of doing something wrong.

To be under a cloud means to be suspected of doing something bad or wrong. It is an idiomatic expression.

(125) (A) He loves to daydream.

To have one's head in the clouds is an idiom that describes people who always believe in unrealistic things.

(126) (D) The man is a small part of a big company.

A small cog in a large wheel is an idiomatic expression that means that the man is a small part of a larger company.

(127) (B) He was ignored.

To be left in the cold means to be ignored.

(128) (C) He criticized the plans.

To pour cold water on is an idiom that means to find faults in a person's plans or suggestions.

(129) (A) It resulted in a crisis.

To bring an issue to a head means that the issue has gotten to the crisis level.

(130) (A) Was.

The correct sentence is: *The manager, as well as his assistant, was here last week.*

This is a question on concord. The first subject determines the verb to be used. The first subject is *the manager* and is in the singular form. The verb, therefore, will be in the singular form.

(131) (D) Anger.

An abstract noun is a noun that cannot be seen or touched but can be felt. Examples of abstract nouns include *air, wind, anger, violence, joy* and *faith*. They are the opposite of concrete nouns, which can be seen, felt and touched.

(132) (A) Girl.

The noun *girl* can take the suffix *-s* to show plurality. These types of nouns are known as regular nouns. The other *options, man, furniture* and *advice,* cannot take the suffix *-s* to show plurality. These are known as mass count nouns. They are nouns that are seen as not having a natural bond. They are also known as uncountable nouns or non-count nouns.

(133) (B) Church.

The noun *church* is a regular noun. The suffix *-es* can be added to the noun *church* to make it plural. For instance, *We saw many churches on our way home.*

(134) (B) Tooth.

Mutation plurals are nouns that become plural by changing one or more letters from their singular form. They do not take the suffixes *-s, -es* or *-is*. Examples of mutation plurals are *mouse–mice* and *louse–lice*. Do not add a suffix to them. Just change the vowels.

(135) (A) Furniture.

Furniture is an example of a mass noun, also known as an uncountable noun. Such nouns always take a singular verb.

(136) (B) Trousers.

Summation plurals are nouns that have two equal parts. Other examples include *glasses, handcuffs, slippers, shoes*. Summation plurals are always followed by plural verbs except when they are preceded by *a pair of* or *the pair of*. In this case, a singular verb is used.

(137) (B) Uncountable noun.

Mass nouns and uncountable nouns are the same. They are used for things that cannot or should not be counted. They are always regarded as singular and are followed by singular verbs. They do not take the suffixes *-s*, *-es* or *-is*. Other examples include *baggage, luggage, advice, water*.

(138) (A) Water.

Water is an example of a mass noun. This is because it cannot be counted except by measuring instruments.

(139) (C) Interested in the information they are imparting.

People will believe almost anything as long as the speaker is sincerely passionate about the information being conveyed.

(140) (B) Understand the audience and their characteristics.

A speaker must study the environment. For instance, the speaker should be able to decide whether the audience is hostile or friendly. The speaker should know the things or activities that are acceptable and unacceptable in the environment. As a Foreign Service officer, you should strive to study the culture of the people who live where you are stationed.

(141) (A) Two to four.

Learn to build eye contact with your audience. It shows that you are confident and truthful. Two to four seconds is enough to establish eye contact with one person.

(142) (A) No person will feel ignored.

Establishing eye contact with everybody will make everybody feel part of the conversation.

(143) (D) Coercion.

Coercion means "force." Force should not be used in attending to conflicts. Resolving conflicts requires the power of words, sound judgment and composure. Respectable leadership and influence are the best way to lead people.

(144) (D) Wisdom/knowledge.

In crisis situations, wisdom and knowledge are very important. Coercion is not needed because it will only worsen the crisis. Be at the same level as the conflicting party/parties. Avoid taking sides. If they are sitting, take a seat. If they are standing, it is best to stand up with them. Listen to what they have to say.

(145) (B) Erroneous.

Hasty judgment will lead to errors. Listen to what others have to say. Do not be in a hurry to make assumptions and pass judgment. Wait until the other parties have finished before you start talking.

(146) (D) Igniting more conflict between parties.

It is not proper for a diplomat to ignite more conflict between parties. Instead, the diplomat should use a calm voice, listen to what both parties have to say and avoid taking sides.

(147) (B) Essential.

Effective communication is an essential life skill that everyone needs to have.

(148) (D) All of the above.

Effective communication is an essential life skill that everyone needs to have. It does not matter whether you are young or old, White or Black, educated or illiterate. Effective communication is not only for those who are in business or the field of communication. Everyone needs to know how to communicate effectively. As a Foreign Service officer, this is a skill you must practice until you gain mastery of it.

(149) (D) None of the above.

Effective communication is an essential life skill that everyone needs to have. It does not matter whether you are young or old, White or Black, educated or illiterate. Effective communication is not only for those who are in business or the field of communication. Everyone needs to know how to communicate effectively. As a Foreign Service officer, this is a skill you must practice until you gain mastery of it.

(150) (D) All of the above.

None of the answers are true about effective speaking. To be a Foreign Service officer who communicates with people effectively, you have to understand and implement some essential communication tools.

(151) (B) It is complex.

Effective speaking is more than just talking or sending your message to an audience. It is a complex process that takes time to learn.

(152) (D) All of the above.

There are specific skills you must develop because they are necessary for keeping your audience interested in your message. When you are speaking effectively, your audience wants to hear more. You will need to connect with your audience through storytelling, entertainment, word choice, the content of your speech and your style of communication.

(153) (C) Confidence.

Confidence is a very important quality when it comes to effective speaking. It makes people see you as an expert, so they're willing to listen to your message.

Test 2: Essay Answer

Prevention of Malaria Is Better Than Cure

According to the World Health Organization (WHO), there were an estimated 229 million malaria cases worldwide in 2019. Malaria was reportedly responsible for 409,000 deaths from these cases. Also, children under five years old, who are considered much more vulnerable due to their developing immune systems, accounted for 67% of the total number of people who died of malaria.

Despite being responsible for the deaths of many people every year, malaria is a preventable disease. Over the years, medical professionals have dedicated their time and intellectual resources to producing drugs and designing programs to improve access to malaria treatment. All of these efforts have been helpful. However, placing our focus on prevention methods is better than wasting resources on curing the disease. Prevention would help reduce the incidence and impact of malaria in Sub-Saharan Africa. It would reduce the number of people who get infected and need to wait to treat the disease after infection.

In 1955, WHO organized the billion-dollar Global Malaria Eradication Programme. With the proposed intention of eliminating malaria in Africa within the next ten years, the program focused on using chloroquine and insecticides to cure and prevent malaria. In 1969, the program was considered unsuccessful, as the number of people in Sub-Saharan Africa who died of malaria increased by over 10% while the program was active. The program's failure hinged on insufficient funds and a lack of infrastructure to support such capital-intensive projects. A program that required more money, infrastructure and expertise than what was obtainable in Sub-Saharan African countries could not be successful.

Furthermore, the extensive use of chloroquine to cure malaria in the past led to the emergence of drug-resistant parasites. The inconsistent use of chloroquine resulted in over 95% of mosquitoes developing resistance, thus exposing more people to the risk of contracting the disease. Since chloroquine has been proven inefficient, newer drugs have been produced to cure malaria, thus increasing the cost of treating the life-threatening disease.

Preventing malaria is cheaper and more proactive, effective and efficient than treating it. A strict focus on preventing malaria will yield positive results by reducing malaria infections and deaths. One of the cheapest and most effective ways of preventing malaria is the use of bed nets as a protective barrier. Insecticide-treated bed nets (ITNs) are much more helpful because mosquitoes get trapped and eventually die, which helps reduce the mosquito population in a community. These nets could be distributed for free or made available and affordable to allow most people to own them. They could reduce the number of malaria parasite transmissions during the night by as much as 90%.

Educating people on simple steps to prevent female anopheles mosquitoes from increasing their populations could also be helpful. These steps include clearing the bushes in the surroundings; cleaning drainages and stagnant water, which serve as breeding sites for mosquitoes; installing screens/nets on windows and wearing protective clothing when outside.

Losing a massive chunk of the population to malaria is unproductive for the area's economy. Having its able-bodied workforce bedridden because of malaria results in loss of work and school days. If we want to build a productive and robust workforce and economy, prevention remains the most effective way of combating this deadly but preventable disease.

Test 3: Job Knowledge Questions

(1) The United States was founded in what year?

(A) 1780

(B) 1873

(C) 1776

(D) 1765

(2) What branch of the government has the duty to create laws?

(A) Legislature

(B) Executive

(C) Judiciary

(D) All of the above

(3) Judges are appointed by _____.

(A) The president

(B) The Congress

(C) The Senate

(D) The chief judge

(4) The legislative branch of the United States government is _____.

(A) Unicameral

(B) Bicameral

(C) Multicameral

(D) Non-representative

(5) House of Representative members serve _____ year(s) per term.

(A) Five

(B) Three

(C) One

(D) Two

(6) How many Senate seats does the United States government have?

(A) 50

(B) 100

(C) 82

(D) 153

(7) The 46th president of the United States is _____.

(A) Donald Trump

(B) Joe Biden

(C) Barack Obama

(D) Bill Clinton

(8) The towns of New England practice _____.

(A) Direct democracy

(B) Representative democracy

(C) Conservative government

(D) Multi-party system

(9) The US government purchased Louisiana from France in what year?

(A) 1776

(B) 1803

(C) 1856

(D) 1987

(10) Slavery in the United States was abolished in what year?

(A) 1765

(B) 1789

(C) 1834

(D) 1865

(11) Which of the following statements is true of the United States during World War I?

(A) It originally took a neutral stance.

(B) It declared war against Germany in 1917.

(C) It supported the Allies in 1918.

(D) All of the above.

(12) Which of the following were bombed by the United States in 1945?

(A) Hiroshima and Nagasaki

(B) Italy and Germany

(C) Japan and Italy

(D) All of the above

(13) Which of the following regions is a major influencer of American culture?

(A) Northern Europe

(B) Africa

(C) South America

(D) France

(14) Which significant act was in force between 1882 and 1943?

(A) The Migration of Africans Act

(B) The Ban on Indian Hemp Act

(C) The Chinese Exclusion Act

(D) The Opening of US Borders Act

(15) Which of the following sports is foremost in American culture?

(A) Baseball

(B) Basketball

(C) Ice hockey

(D) Football

(16) The biggest denomination of religious groups in the United States is
_____.

(A) Catholic

(B) Protestant

(C) Muslim

(D) Jew

(17) Which of the following is true in US foreign policy?

(A) It is not mandatory for the United States to abide by all policies the world supports.

(B) The United States must agree with the policies to which five major powers consent.

(C) If it does not suit the interests of the United States, the United States is still obligated to support such agreements.

(D) Americans living in or investing abroad are in danger.

(18) The relationship between the United States and Europe is based on what model?

(A) Hub and spoke

(B) Bilateral

(C) Multilateral

(D) Unilateral

(19) Two-thirds of the world's oil reserves are in _____.

(A) Texas

(B) Egypt

(C) Russia

(D) The Persian Gulf

(20) A key aspect of the international relations of the State Department is _____.

(A) Foreign aid

(B) International disputes

(C) Closing the United States border

(D) Establishing tariffs

(21) The Treasury Department oversees _____.

(A) State budgets

(B) Annual income of the federal government

(C) Bilateral economic assistance

(D) Multilateral assistance

(22) NATO is a collaboration of how many European and North American nations?

(A) 12

(B) 29

(C) 18

(D) 34

(23) The position of the United States in the United Nations Security Council is _____.

(A) Permanent

(B) Elected

(C) Temporary

(D) For three decades

(24) The United States often uses _____ to carry out covert operations.

(A) WTO

(B) State police

(C) The CIA

(D) Homeland Security

(25) When did Christopher Columbus's voyages begin?

(A) 1490

(B) 1491

(C) 1492

(D) 1493

(26) What disrupted the millennia of independent indigenous existence in South America?

(A) European colonization by Spain and Portugal

(B) African colonization by Egypt

(C) European colonization by Italy and France

(D) European colonization by England and Germany

(27) When did Europe experience human influxes from the east and southeast?

(A) During the Neolithic era

(B) During the modern era

(C) During the Paleolithic era

(D) During the Middle ages

(28) When did the United Kingdom leave the European Union?

(A) January 31, 2019

(B) January 31, 2020

(C) January 31, 2018

(D) March 31, 2021

(29) What led to the age of Islamic gunpowder empires?

(A) The English Renaissance

(B) The American Revolution

(C) The French Revolution

(D) The Timurid Renaissance

(30) From what part of the world did Islam spread into Africa?

(A) Istanbul

(B) Afghanistan

(C) Arabia

(D) Timbuktu

(31) From where did indigenous Australians first arrive?

(A) Southwest Asia

(B) Southeast Asia

(C) North Asia

(D) Asia

(32) On whose side did Australia fight during the world wars?

(A) Germany

(B) Japan

(C) Great Britain

(D) Austria

(33) The Foreign Service is overseen by a _____.

(A) Director general

(B) Lieutenant

(C) Colonel

(D) Major general

(34) The first director general of the Foreign Service was _____.

(A) Selden Chapin

(B) Joshua Brian

(C) Carlos Perez

(D) Joe Turner

(35) The Foreign Service was formed in what year?

(A) 1957

(B) 1945

(C) 1924

(D) 1912

(36) How many diplomatic bases does the United States have all over the world?

(A) 651

(B) 193

(C) 349

(D) 265

(37) The Foreign Commerce Service was created in _____.

(A) 1967

(B) 1954

(C) 2001

(D) 1927

(38) Alien personnel is the same as _____.

(A) Foreign Service reservists

(B) Locally employed staff

(C) Chiefs of mission

(D) Consular agents

(39) Foreign Service nationals (FSNs) _____.

(A) Were once called third-country nationals (TCNs)

(B) Are locally employed staff (LE staff)

(C) Are non-Americans living in other countries

(D) Are not members of the Foreign Service

(40) Clientitis is _____.

(A) A client without regard for diplomats

(B) A situation in which a diplomat tends to refer to the officials and citizens from the host countries by the term *clients*

(C) A client of the host country

(D) An investor seeking to invest in a foreign country

(41) _____ is used for locating users on the internet.

(A) The IP address

(B) Domain Name System (DNS)

(C) Uniform Resource Identifiers (URIs)

(D) Hypertext Transfer Protocol (HTTP)

(42) We use computers to _____.

(A) Make our tasks easier and faster

(B) Feed the poor

(C) Increase the national wealth of the United States

(D) Replace humans

(43) The motherboard is an example of _____.

(A) Hardware

(B) Software

(C) Operating systems

(D) Information

(44) _____ is/are used to send data into the computer.

(A) Senders

(B) Google Chrome

(C) Data installers

(D) Input devices

(45) Monitors, printers and video cards are _____.

(A) Software

(B) Control units

(C) Input devices

(D) Output devices

(46) The combination of the ALU, the control unit and registers collectively forms the _____.

(A) Motherboard

(B) Central processing unit

(C) Output device

(D) Input devices

(47) A device that helps with data inputting, editing, formatting and production or output of text is called a/an_____.

(A) Text explorer

(B) Editor

(C) File formatter

(D) Word processor

(48) The organized and systematic collection of data that is stored in the computer system is called _____.

(A) Storage

(B) Database

(C) Desktop publishing

(D) Spreadsheet

(49) Isaac and Victor are planning a birthday party. They have made arrangements to have 25 bottles of wine for their 50 guests. All of a sudden, they are told 30 guests will be attending the party. How many bottles will they now need altogether?

(A) 20

(B) 30

(C) 40

(D) 50

(50) A Catholic who earns $3,000 every month tithes 10% of his income. How much is this?

(A) $30

(B) $50

(C) $300

(D) $3

(51) X + 5 = 50. Find X.

(A) 12

(B) 55

(C) 45

(D) 65

(52) What is the median of this set of ages? 43, 34, 56, 83, 25, 67, 90

(A) 34

(B) 56

(C) 83

(D) 67

(53) A natural resource that includes the earth's surface and water bodies is
_____.

(A) Land

(B) Labor

(C) Capital

(D) Enterprise

(54) Cash in hand, loans and overdrafts are referred to as _____.

(A) Fixed assets

(B) Temporary assets

(C) Circulating assets

(D) Solid assets

(55) Which law states that when there is an increase in the utility of a factor of production while other factors remain constant, there will be an increase in return of production, followed by a fall?

(A) The law of uprising

(B) The law of upthrust

(C) The law of diminishing returns

(D) The law of elasticity

(56) A business that comprises the resources of two to 20 individuals in its establishment and operations is a _____.

(A) Sole proprietorship

(B) Partnership

(C) Joint-stock company

(D) Public limited liability company

(57) The quantity of goods and services consumers are willing and have the capacity to buy at a defined price and time is _____.

(A) Demand

(B) Desire

(C) Want

(D) Need

(58) When goods and services are demanded because of the demand for other products, it is called _____ demand.

(A) Complementary

(B) Composite

(C) Competitive

(D) Derived

(59) A market system that requires private control of properties is _____.

(A) Capitalism

(B) Socialism

(C) Communism

(D) Public economy

(60) Hungary, Yugoslavia, Soviet Union and China are referred to as _____ states.

(A) Communist

(B) Capitalist

(C) Monarchical

(D) Monopolistic

Test 3: Situational Judgment Questions

(61) You have been asked to draft a 50-page document for your department in a very short amount of time. The best way to approach this task is to _____.

(A) Start the job as soon as possible

(B) Give the work to whoever is available to finish the task

(C) Work beyond office hours to meet deadlines

(D) Identify those who are skilled in this area and divide the task into roles

(62) A quality Foreign Service administration requires that _____.

(A) Everyone stands as the authority

(B) The authority understands its responsibilities and executes them with reservations

(C) There be room for questioning

(D) There be a vast communication gap

(63) If you plan to excel in the Foreign Service, _____.

(A) You will need discipline.

(B) You don't need to worry about collaborating.

(C) You can procrastinate occasionally.

(D) Honesty is unimportant.

(64) Those in authority should _____.

(A) Interfere with the affairs of employees who are not directly below them

(B) Act superior and be judgmental

(C) Avoid meddling in the matters of those who are not directly below them

(D) Stay away from employees

(65) Your Foreign Service goals should be _____.

(A) Specific

(B) Immeasurable

(C) Irrelevant to the central focus

(D) Countless

(66) Whose interest should you serve while in the Foreign Service?

(A) Your family's

(B) Your ambition's

(C) Your religion's

(D) Your country's

(67) Non-financial rewards include _____.

(A) A day off

(B) Praise

(C) Recognition

(D) All of the above

(68) The best way to manage an organization is _____.

(A) A balanced approach to power-sharing

(B) Lopsided power management

(C) Bottom full, top empty

(D) Top full, bottom empty

(69) As a Foreign Service officer, you should not _____.

(A) Worry about who is above you

(B) Work in the office

(C) Have access to your superiors

(D) Work without following the hierarchy of structure

(70) Which of the following is not true about the workplace environment?

(A) Disorderliness will lead to frustration.

(B) Arrangement of the work environment should boost the morale of officers.

(C) Employees need to be psychologically sound.

(D) Efficiency does not demand orderliness.

(71) Muslims in the workplace or in the field _____.

(A) Should be treated with suspicion

(B) Should not be promoted to certain top levels of an organization

(C) Are likely to plan terrorist attacks

(D) Should be treated with equity

(72) _____ is/are a way of increasing stability in the workplace.

(A) Job security

(B) Penalties

(C) Reduction of salaries

(D) Cutting of workers' remuneration

(73) _____ is the hallmark of exceptional Foreign Service officers.

(A) Initiative

(B) Curiosity

(C) Strength

(D) Kindness

(74) There should be _____ and _____ in the workplace.

(A) Anger/envy

(B) Compassion/over-ambition

(C) Self-gratification/loyalty to the mission

(D) None of the above

(75) _____ is a feeling of oneness shared among members of the same group who are pursuing one goal.

(A) Esprit de corps

(B) Sincerity

(C) Truth

(D) All of the above

(76) Which of the following is the best way to influence a Foreign Service officer to improve his or her work?

(A) Monetary reward

(B) Queries

(C) Threats

(D) Ease of task

(77) What should be your motive when at a negotiation table?

(A) Strive to be a winner who takes all.

(B) Make your interests obvious as soon as the negotiation begins.

(C) Seek to put other negotiators at a disadvantage.

(D) Try to ensure everyone goes home a winner.

(78) What should you do when the workload becomes too much for you to handle?

(A) Quit.

(B) Outsource tasks to outsiders.

(C) Respectfully tell your boss it is too much to handle.

(D) Do the task as best as you can.

(79) You are having some family issues and are finding it difficult to concentrate at work. What should you do?

(A) Ask for a few days off.

(B) Visit a counselor.

(C) Act like nothing is wrong.

(D) Quit so that you can focus on your home life.

(80) Which of the following people should be your priority when on a diplomatic mission if you have to choose?

(A) The old

(B) The women

(C) The children

(D) The youth

(81) You have a partner who is a sanguine. How should you relate to her?

(A) Be hostile to her sometimes.

(B) Avoid getting close to her.

(C) Do not relay sensitive, confidential information to her.

(D) Work with her very warily.

(82) When a choleric has made up his mind about pursuing a vision, but you feel it is a waste of time, what should you do?

(A) Forget about the plan.

(B) Fight against the vision.

(C) Be practical when dissuading the officer.

(D) Force him to stop.

(83) When it comes to phlegmatics, you should _____.

(A) Expect them to mistrust you at first

(B) Know they will rarely talk much to you

(C) Be aware their loyalty is often unquestionable

(D) All of the above

(84) Melancholics expect you to be _____.

(A) Shallow minded

(B) Carefree

(C) Knowledgeable about your opinions

(D) Unhappy

(85) There are generally _____ types of people you are likely to come across while working as a diplomat.

(A) Three

(B) Four

(C) Five

(D) Six

(86) Everyone in the organization should be pursuing _____.

(A) Similar goals

(B) Different goals

(C) Personal goals

(D) None of the above

(87) Which should you put first?

(A) The United States

(B) Your home country

(C) Your family

(D) All of the above

(88) Which of the following is a form of reward?

(A) Praise

(B) Promotion

(C) A day off

(D) All of the above

Test 3; English Expression Questions

Usage of English: Passage 3

(1) Artificial Intelligence, which is also known as AI, is an aspect of software engineering built to perform the functions of humans. (2) AI is integrated into other disciplines, and it <u>commonly</u> has diverse methodologies. (3) AI is practically impacting almost every field of human endeavors. (4) We can see it in medicine, education, transportation, social media, administration and other sectors of our modern society.

(5) Almost a decade after the Nazi encryption <u>Technology</u> Enigma was decrypted and the Allied forces were able to win World War II, Alan Turing changed history when he began exploring machines' ability to think. (6) AI is the answer to Turing's question because it is the imitation of human intelligence and problem-solving skills.

(7) Norvig and Russell have investigated four methods of characterizing AI technology—humane thinking, sane thinking, humane actions and reasonable actions. (8) The first two categorizations make reference to thought, while the latter two focus on the conduct of AI technology. (9) This categorization is a reference to every scientist who wishes to undertake the study and invention of intelligent machines. (10) Is<u> there any other definition of AI?</u>

(11) Ford educator Patrick Winston defines AI with computer terminologies. (12) He describes AI as imperatively induced calculations that help machines think, discern and perform regular tasks. <u>(13) Although these definitions may be quite technical for laymen to understand. (14) They are pivotal to the </u>foundations of AI in the field of software engineering. (15) They are the fundamentals that guide the dynamic inquiries and activities of scientists when building AI machines.

(89) Which of the following is most suitable for replacing the underlined word in sentence 2?

(A) Often

(B) Seldom

(C) However

(D) Likely

(90) What should be done to the underlined word in sentence 5?

(A) Leave it like that.

(B) Make every letter lowercase.

(C) Capitalize all the letters.

(D) Make the initial letter lowercase.

(91) What should be replaced in sentence 10?

(A) Nothing

(B) The pronoun

(C) The question

(D) The adjective

(92) What needs to be replaced in sentences 13 and 14?

(A) The dependent clause

(B) The independent clause

(C) The subject

(D) The period

(93) According to the passage, what characterizes AI?

(A) Thinking humanly

(B) Thinking logically

(C) Acting humanly

(D) All of the above

Sentence Selection

(94) Choose the sentence that is most suitable for standard written English.

(A) When I was traveling, after the examination had ended, I met a kind woman.

(B) I met a kind woman on my way from the examination.

(C) After the examination had ended, when I was traveling I met a kind woman.

(D) When I was traveling after the examination had ended, I met a kind woman.

(95) Choose the sentence that is most suitable for standard written English.

(A) The buildings we're demolished ten years ago; although we can still see some parts of them.

(B) The buildings were demolished ten years ago, although we can still see some parts of them.

(C) The buildings we're demolished ten years ago: although we can yet see some parts of them.

(D) The buildings were demolished ten years ago, although we can still see some parts of them.

(96) Choose the sentence that is most suitable for standard written English.

(A) Oh you have finally been employed in the Foreign Service department.

(B) Oh! You have finally been employed in the Foreign Service department.

(C) Oh you have finally been employed! In the Foreign Service department.

(D) Oh you have finally been employed in the Foreign Service department.

Sentence Correction

For each sentence, choose the underlined word(s) that should be replaced to correct the sentence, or identify if there are no errors.

(97) Allen, <u>which</u> car <u>was stolen</u> last week, has been <u>given</u> a new car.

(A) No errors

(B) which

(C) was stolen

(D) given

(98) <u>The director general</u> with his wife <u>is</u> celebrating <u>his birthday.</u>

(A) No errors

(B) The director general

(C) is

(D) his birthday

(99) <u>A number of</u> parents <u>was here</u> yesterday, but they have all gone back to <u>their homes</u>.

(A) No errors

(B) A number of

(C) was here

(D) their homes

(100) <u>Can</u> you please tell the teacher to give him <u>is</u> big book <u>which</u> is on the shelf?

(A) No errors

(B) Can

(C) is

(D) which

(101) When I <u>checked</u> the time again, I noticed that the cattle <u>has been grazing</u> in the field for <u>approximately</u> six hours.

(A) No errors

(B) has been grazing

(C) checked

(D) approximately

Paragraph Organization

(102) Choose the clearest and most organized sentence arrangement.

Sentence 1: The internet is an electronic network that allows millions of people across the globe to share information.

Sentence 2: The internet has many advantages and disadvantages.

Sentence 3: Some children watch violent and pornographic films on the internet.

Sentence 4: Parents should offer guidance to their children.

(A) 1, 2, 3, 4

(B) 1, 2, 4, 3

(C) 3, 2, 1, 4

(D) 4, 1, 2, 3

(103) Choose the clearest and most organized sentence arrangement.

Sentence 1: Many developing countries are facing the challenge of high unemployment.

Sentence 2: Unemployment is when there is unutilized labor that could have been engaged for productivity.

Sentence 3: Another cause of unemployment is the abandonment of the economy's agricultural sector.

Sentence 4: There are various reasons for the increase in unemployment.

(A) 2, 1, 4, 3

(B) 1, 2, 4, 3

(C) 1, 2, 3, 4

(D) 2, 1, 3, 4

(104) Choose the clearest and most organized sentence arrangement.

Sentence 1: Bribery and corruption is the illegal offering of money or non-monetary valuables to influence the decision of someone in authority.

Sentence 2: It is a social menace that can be found in public service.

Sentence 3: Furthermore, bribery and corruption can be found in the educational sector.

Sentence 4: There are opinions that bribery and corruption can be stopped in agencies, government and executives.

(A) 1, 2, 3, 4

(B) 4, 3, 2, 1

(C) 1, 2, 4, 3

(D) 2, 3, 1, 4

(105) Choose the clearest and most organized sentence arrangement.

Sentence 1: Immunization is a way of preventing diseases by injecting specially treated disease-causing organisms into the body.

Sentence 2: Most diseases are contagious; that is, they are communicable from one person to another.

Sentence 3: Immunization usually begins from the days of pregnancy and shortly after birth.

Sentence 4: The terms *vaccination* and *inoculation* may be used to mean *immunization*.

(A) 2, 1, 4, 3

(B) 1, 2, 4, 3

(C) 1, 2, 3, 4

(D) 2, 1, 3, 4

(106) Choose the clearest and most organized sentence arrangement.

Sentence 1: Patriotism is how we show that we love our country and will be ready to serve it.

Sentence 2: Being patriotic also means respecting national identity.

Sentence 3: If Americans are called to serve their country in times of war or peace, they should be ready to serve.

Sentence 4: As citizens of America, we should be loyal to our state and federal governments.

(A) 1, 2, 3, 4

(B) 1, 3, 4, 2

(C) 1, 2, 4, 3

(D) 1, 3, 4, 2

Paragraph Revision

Study these sentences and answer the questions that come after them.

Sentence 1: In the last fifty years, scientists have made notable advancements in genetic engineering.

Sentence 2: Scientists are now close to the point of redesigning the human body to improve its function.

Sentence 3: The greatest advantage of genetic engineering is found in agriculture.

Sentence 4: However, there are some grave <u>danger</u> of genetic engineering.

(107) This sentence has been omitted from the above list: *Several scientists have postulated that HIV was a result of mistaken genetic engineering.* What sentence should this be inserted after?

(A) Sentence 1

(B) Sentence 2

(C) Sentence 3

(D) Sentence 4

(108) What word will most suitably replace the underlined item in sentence 4?

(A) Dangers

(B) Dangerous

(C) Limitation

(D) Disadvantage

Choose the correct answer.

(109) The professor did several _____ on the topic.

(A) Analysis

(B) Analyses

(C) Analy's

(D) Analyes

(110) I dropped by _____ Wednesday.

(A) at

(B) by

(C) on

(D) in

(111) The girls _____ danced today.

(A) Have

(B) Has

(C) Haved

(D) Has'

(112) Jacob and Andrew _____ fighting.

(A) Are

(B) Is

(C) Was

(D) Have

(113) The man is _____ the office.

(A) On

(B) On top

(C) In

(D) With

(114) Gymnastics _____ my favorite sport.

(A) Were

(B) Are

(C) Is

(D) Am

(115) The passengers, along with the bus driver, _____ been kidnapped.

(A) Have

(B) Has

(C) Was

(D) Is

(116) Singing _____ a nice activity.

(A) Are

(B) Is

(C) Were

(D) Weren't

(117) The women who came here _____ helped by the commissioner.

(A) Was

(B) Is

(C) Were

(D) has

(118) That man who is standing there _____ my teacher.

(A) Is

(B) Were

(C) Are

(D) Weren't

(119) The kidnappers _____ been arrested.

(A) Have

(B) Has

(C) Are

(D) Is

(120) He gave _____ the book.

(A) We

(B) I

(C) Us

(D) Their

(121) That book is _____.

(A) Theirs

(B) Their

(C) Your

(D) My

(122) Which of the following expressions is correct?

(A) The book is my.

(B) The book is mine.

(C) The book is your.

(D) The book is our.

(123) I ran _____ the road.

(A) With

(B) At

(C) Outside

(D) Across

(124) To be a good man _____ not easy.

(A) Were

(B) Is

(C) Are

(D) Weren't

(125) _____ *faithfully* is a complimentary close used in a formal letter.

(A) Yours

(B) Your

(C) You're

(D) Your's

(126) My friends _____ to the cinema every weekend.

(A) Go

(B) Goes

(C) Gone

(D) Goes's

(127) Phonetics and phonology _____ difficult to study.

(A) Are

(B) Were

(C) Weren't

(D) Is

(128) The commissioner of education, in the company of some principals, _____ carrying out inspections on schools

(A) Is

(B) Are

(C) Were

(D) Aren't

(129) The number of school principals in the country _____ one hundred.

(A) Are

(B) Were

(C) Is

(D) Have been

(130) Either the principal or the teachers _____ in school by now.

(A) Are

(B) Was

(C) Is

(D) Isn't

(131) The kind man helped Kola and _____.

(A) I

(B) She

(C) Me

(D) We

(132) My father and _____ saw the fight that took place in the market.

(A) Me

(B) Us

(C) I

(D) Them

(133) Reading the Bible _____ one grow spiritually.

(A) Make

(B) Makes

(C) Makes'

(D) Make's

(134) I gave you a ruler yesterday. You broke _____.

(A) Him

(B) It's

(C) Its'

(D) It

(135) _____ high time we left this place.

(A) It's

(B) It

(C) Its'

(D) Its

(136) I have _____ the book.

(A) Saw

(B) Seen

(C) See

(D) Seeing

(137) Last week, he had _____ to help us.

(A) Promised

(B) Promise

(C) Promises

(D) Promising

(138) The clergy _____ here.

(A) Is

(B) Are

(C) Was

(D) Isn't

(139) Which Foreign Service officer will the people believe?

(A) The one who does not know what he is saying.

(B) The one who is very sure of what he is saying.

(C) The one who is ambivalent.

(D) All of the above.

(140) Before you speak on a foreign policy as a US delegate, _____.

(A) You must have traveled to other countries.

(B) You must have been in the Foreign Service department for 29 years.

(C) You must have served as the director general.

(D) You must be totally convinced that it is right.

(141) _____ is what will make you go to any length to speak in favor of US foreign policies.

(A) Hatred for your country

(B) Desire for your country

(C) Your ultimate need

(D) Passion for your country

(142) Which of the following statements is true about any audience?

(A) They know everything that you are about to say.

(B) They are ready to laugh at you for any slight error.

(C) They do not have long attention spans.

(D) They want to ridicule you.

(143) What should you do when communicating with an audience for 30 minutes?

(A) Make sure no one else is talking.

(B) Stand in the middle of the crowd.

(C) Have an open debate of the topic after 7 to 15 minutes.

(D) Divide your speech into segments and give room for the audience to participate, contribute and ask questions.

(144) When your audience is involved in the communication process, _____.

(A) It will lead to too much noise.

(B) It may lead to a quarrel.

(C) They are less likely to give their attention to something else.

(D) No one will be able to stop them.

(145) What is the effect of wordiness on your listeners?

(A) It improves their understanding.

(B) It expands their vocabulary.

(C) It makes the points easier to understand.

(D) It may make your audience forget the key points you are trying to impart.

(146) Humans love _____.

(A) Pain

(B) Crises

(C) Entertainment

(D) Mysteries

(147) Effective communication should _____.

(A) Be straightforward and don't use stories.

(B) Give listeners the pleasure of hearing a story.

(C) Utilize your time and ignore whether the listeners are stressed or not.

(D) State the facts and be very formal.

(148) Which of the following is true about storytelling?

(A) It is a source of distraction to listeners.

(B) It wastes time.

(C) It helps people retain information.

(D) It should always be nonfiction.

(149) Trying to understand your listeners' cultural, educational, political and social background is called _____.

(A) Political consciousness

(B) Religious consciousness

(C) Educational consciousness

(D) Environmental consciousness

(150) If you are sent to be an ambassador in a foreign nation, _____.

(A) You should get some books to study about the people you will be interacting with.

(B) Go online to read up about other people's experiences.

(C) Look for a friendly local who can explain what you should expect.

(D) All of the above.

(151) Which of the following matters in communication?

(A) The time

(B) The place

(C) The message

(D) All of the above

(152) Which of the following is not ideal in effective speaking?

(A) Planning your speech

(B) Keeping reminder notes

(C) Constant repetition

(D) Not listing your key points

(153) When trying to articulate your message with the best impact, _____.

(A) Be clear with your articulation.

(B) Don't use anecdotes.

(C) Keep the volume of your voice low.

(D) All of the above.

Test 3: Essay Question

There is an ongoing debate regarding the necessity of capital punishment. The argument is about whether it is necessary and whether corrupt public officers should face stiff penalties. In your view, do you think public officers deserve severe legal punishment if they are found on the wrong side of the law?

Test 3: Job Knowledge Answers and Explanations

(1) (C) 1776.

The federal government of the United States is a republic located on the North American continent. It is made of 50 states, 14 independent territories and islands, one federal district and 15 departments. It was founded in 1776.

The three branches of the US government are the legislature, the executive and the judiciary.

(2) (A) Legislature.

It is the duty of the legislature to create laws. However, the executive may decide to veto the bills of the legislation, while Congress may unite and override the acts of the executive. The Supreme Court also has the power to vitiate the laws the legislature has created.

(3) (A) The president.

It is the duty of the president to nominate judges, which must also pass the scrutiny and approval of the Supreme Court, which is the number one judiciary body in the United States. This is an act of checks and balances within the US government.

(4) (B) Bicameral.

The legislative branch of the United States is also known as Congress. Congress is bicameral. It has the responsibility of creating laws that are approved by the president. This means that it is made of two houses: the House of Representatives and the Senate.

(5) (D) Two.

The House of Representatives members serve two years per term. However, there is no limit to how many times a representative can be reelected. Individuals can run for Congress when they are 25 or older.

(6) (B) 100.

There are 100 senators (two senators per state multiplied by 50 states) in the United States. The Senate is unlike the House of Representatives. It includes two senators for every state regardless of a state's population. An elected senator's term is six years. Almost every two years, about a third of the Senate goes up for election.

(7) (B) Joe Biden.

As of January 20, 2021, the president of the executive branch is Joe Biden. He is the 46th president of the United States. The vice president is Kamala Harris. She is the 49th vice president. The establishment and investiture of power upon the executive is seen in Article II of the US Constitution.

(8) (A) Direct democracy.

There is direct democracy in the towns of New England. It functions on the constitutional provisions of tribe government. Some states, like Massachusetts, Rhode Island and Connecticut, do not have counties with much inherent power. However, some counties have so much power that they can receive taxes and pay law enforcement agencies.

(9) (B) 1803.

In 1803, the US government purchased Louisiana from France, and the nation's geographic size doubled. In that era, the United States continued to expand toward the Pacific Coast as its population and economic size continued to grow.

(10) (D) 1865.

Slavery was abolished on December 5, 1865, by the Thirteenth Amendment. This occurred after the Confederacy attacked a federal property in 1861 and the Civil War began. The war ended when the US government defeated the Confederacy in 1865. This led to a Reconstruction era, in which voting and legal rights were given to freed slaves.

(11) (D) All of the above.

At first, the United States took a neutral stance in World War I. Then it declared war against Germany in 1917 and supported the Allies in 1918. The United States' later involvement in World War I was very impactful.

(12) (A) Hiroshima and Nagasaki.

In 1941, when Japan bombed Pearl Harbor, the United States declared war on Japan and joined the Allies. The Allies conquered fascist Italy and Nazi Germany. In 1945 the United States dropped atomic bombs on two cities in Japan, Hiroshima and Nagasaki, ending the war.

(13) (A) Northern Europe.

US society is a western culture that has its own music, dialect, food, games, lifestyle and literature. The values of the United States are secular, rational and self-expressive. It takes after the British culture, which established itself in North

America during the colonial era. As a result, Northern Europe is the major influencer of American culture.

(14) (C) The Chinese Exclusion Act.

From 1882 to 1943, the Chinese Exclusion Act was in force. It banned the immigration of Chinese citizens into America. About 120,000 Americans of Japanese descent were jailed in internment camps during World War II. African Americans and Hispanics are not the only people who have been discriminated against in American history.

(15) (A) Baseball.

Baseball is considered the foremost sport in the United States. Basketball, ice hockey and American football are also popular. For a time, horse racing and boxing captured the American people's attention. However, golf and auto racing have taken over. Tennis is also another popular outdoor activity in the United States.

(16) (A) Catholic.

About 74% of Americans are Christians, with 49% Protestant. Twenty-nine percent of Americans identify themselves as Catholics, which makes Catholicism the biggest denomination in the United States. Protestants are subdivided into other smaller denominations, whereas Catholicism is a single unit. Other religious sects in the United States include Judaism, Islam, Buddhism and Hinduism. About 18% of Americans are not religious. They are atheists and agnostics.

(17) (A) It is not mandatory for the United States to abide by all policies the world supports.

It is not in the foreign policy of the United States to compulsorily participate in all agreements that the international community agrees to and abides by. It does not matter whether advanced countries or the majority of countries in the world are in agreement. If it does not suit the interests of the United States, then the United States is not obligated to support such agreements.

(18) (C) Multilateral.

The relationship between the United States and Europe was built on a multilateral model. An example is NATO. However, the international relationship between the United States and Asia is built on a hub and spoke model, which uses bilateral agreements between individual nations and the United States.

(19) (D) The Persian Gulf.

Most of the world's oil reserves, about two-thirds, are believed to be in the Persian Gulf. During World War II, the United States identified its interest in this region. Several decades later, the US enacted President Jimmy Carter's doctrine, which made it clear that when necessary, the United States would use military force to secure its national interest in the Persian Gulf area.

(20) (A) Foreign aid.

The United States offers foreign aid to nations and institutions all over the world. Foreign aid is a key aspect of the State Department's international relations. It is entrenched in US foreign policy. As of 2014, the budget for international affairs was $49 billion.

(21) (D) Multilateral assistance.

The Treasury Department oversees multilateral assistance. However, the US Agency for International Development (USAID) is in charge of most of the bilateral economic assistance the United States offers. In 2014, $23 billion in international donations made the United States the biggest foreign donor.

(22) (B) 29.

The United States is one of the pioneers of NATO, which is a collaboration of 29 European and North American nations. In the heat of the Cold War, NATO was established to secure Western Europe against the Soviet Union. The NATO treaty compels the United States to fight alongside any nation under NATO when there is an external attack.

(23) (A) Permanent.

Ever since World War II, the United States has held a permanent position in the United Nations Security Council. It also wields veto power. Since the fall of the Soviet Union, the United States has remained the world's foremost superpower.

(24) (C) The CIA.

One US foreign policy is the use of covert operations to displace foreign governments that oppose the interests of the United States. The United States often uses the Central Intelligence Agency (CIA) to carry out its covert operations. The State and Naval Departments are sometimes involved in these covert operations.

(25) (C) 1492.

With the age of exploration and Christopher Columbus's voyages (starting in 1492), Europeans started arriving in North America in large numbers and developed colonial ambitions for both North and South America. The "discovery" of America by Columbus is a controversial idea because the Americas were already largely populated by Native Americans, who had developed distinctive civilizations in their own right.

(26) (D) European colonization by England and Germany.

Millennia of independent indigenous existence in South America was disrupted by European colonization by Spain and Portugal and by demographic collapse. This disruption is what created the present framework of cultures in South America.

(27) (A) During the Neolithic era.

During the Neolithic era and the Indo-European migrations, Europe witnessed human influxes from the east and southeast, as well as subsequent crucial cultural and material exchange. The period known as classical antiquity started with the emergence of ancient Greek city-states. Later, the Roman Empire became dominant in the entire Mediterranean basin. The fall of the Roman Empire in the year AD 476 traditionally marks the beginning of the Middle Ages.

(28) (B) January 31, 2020.

In June 2016, 52% of United Kingdom voters voted to leave the European Union, leading to the complicated Brexit separation process and negotiations, which then led to political and economic changes for both the United Kingdom and the remaining EU countries. The United Kingdom eventually left the EU on January 31, 2020.

(29) (D) The Timurid Renaissance.

With the spread of Islam came the Islamic Golden Age and the Timurid Renaissance, which led to the age of Islamic gunpowder empires. Another major achievement was the creation of gunpowder in medieval China, later developed by the gunpowder empires, mostly by the Mughals and Safavids, which led to advanced warfare.

(30) (C) Arabia.

During the Middle Ages, Islam spread west from Arabia to Egypt, crossing the Maghreb and the Sahel. After the desertification of the Sahara, North Africa's history became intertwined with the Middle East and Southern Europe, while the Bantu expansion began from modern-day Cameroon and continued across much of the Sub-Saharan continent in waves between around 1000 BC and AD 1.

(31) (B) Southeast Asia.

Indigenous Australians arrived on the Australian mainland by sea from Southeast Asia from 50,000 to 65,000 years ago.

(32) (C) Great Britain.

In 1901, the colonies carried out a vote, and the majority agreed to form a federation that established modern Australia. Australia fought with Great Britain in both world wars and formed a long-term alliance with the United States when it was threatened during World War II by Imperial Japan.

(33) (A) Director general.

The Foreign Service is superintended by a director general. Currently, Carol Perez is the director general of the Foreign Service. The position of the director general of the Foreign Service is obtained by appointment of the president with the suggestion and approval of the Senate.

(34) (A) Selden Chapin.

From 1946 to 1980, the secretary of state appointed the director general. The first director general of the Foreign Service was Selden Chapin. He was in office for just six months before Christian Ravndal was appointed to replace him. Christian Ravndal stayed in office as the director general until 1949.

(35) (C) 1924.

The Foreign Service was formed in 1924 through the Rogers Act. It was made to be a single administrative unit that combines all diplomatic and consular services as one. The Rogers Act states that it is through the Foreign Service system that the US secretary of state sends diplomats to other nations.

(36) (D) 265.

Foreign Service officers are assigned to one of the 265 US diplomatic bases all over the world. These diplomatic missions include consulates, embassies and other US facilities. To be selected to serve the United States as a Foreign Service officer, you need to pass different written and oral assessments.

(37) (D) 1927.

The Foreign Commerce Service was created in 1927 when Congress passed the legislation that gave a diplomatic credential to representatives of the Department of Commerce in other nations. Another such law was passed in 1930 in the agricultural extension. It established the Foreign Agricultural Service from the Department of Agriculture.

(38) (B) Locally employed staff.

Alien personnel were once called Foreign Service nationals, then they were called locally employed staff. When the Department of State made the request, the US Congress in 1946 passed a Foreign Service act that established six categories of employees—Foreign Service officers, chiefs of mission, Foreign Service reservists, Foreign Service staff, consular agents and alien personnel.

(39) (A) Were once called third-country nationals (TCNs).

Foreign Service nationals (FSNs) are personnel whose duties are administrative, technical, clerical and fiscal across various countries. They may be natives of the country where they work and were once called third-country nationals (TCNs). According to the Foreign Service Act, they are also regarded as members of the Foreign Service and not locally employed staff (LE staff), who may be Americans living in other countries.

(40) (B) A situation in which a diplomat tends to refer to the officials and citizens from the host countries by the term *clients*.

Clientitis is also known as *localitis* or *clientism*. It is a situation in which the resident staff tends to call the officials and citizens from the host country by the term *clients*. This is seen in businesses and governments all over the world. It is synonymous with *going native*. To avoid clientitis, the Department of State trains new ambassadors and gives them orientations that warn them about the issue of clientitis.

(41) (A) The IP address.

IP addresses are used for locating users on the internet. They are like your home addresses, which have a number and the street of your home or building. When users want to have access to a website, they input the domain name (such as www.forbes.com) and not the IP address, which is more difficult to remember. The Domain Name System (DNS) converts the domain names into IP, which is more effective.

(42) (A) Make our tasks easier and faster.

Computers make our tasks neater, more organized, and faster. They are meant to take away burdens, not replace humans. A computer is an electronic machine that accepts and processes data, then produces information. Basically, a computer is programmed to automatically work out logical operations.

(43) (A) Hardware.

Hardware includes all the tangible parts of a computer. It consists of the parts we can touch. This includes a motherboard, circuits, cables, computer chips, graphics cards, keyboards, sound cards, printers, displays and memory (RAM). The motherboard is a core aspect of the computer. Without it, the computer is an empty box.

(44) (D) Input devices.

Input devices are used to send data to the computer. The CPU does the processing of the data before it is produced as information through the output device. Examples of input devices include a keyboard, mouse, image scanner, camera, joystick, light pen, touch screen, microphone and trackball.

(45) (D) Output devices.

Output devices produce information after the input device has sent in data for the CPU to process. Examples of input devices are a monitor, printer, video card, projector and speaker.

(46) (B) Central processing unit.

The combination of the ALU, the control unit and registers collectively forms the central processing unit (CPU). The control unit is also called the control system because it organizes or manages the other parts of a computer. It reads then interprets a program's instructions, then changes them into control signals, which activate other components of the computer system.

(47) (D) Word processor.

A word processor is a device that helps with inputting of data, editing, formatting and production or output of text. Word processors are software found in a general computer. A word processor functions as a text editor and desktop publishing. An example is Microsoft Word.

(48) (B) Database.

A database is the organized and systematic collection of data that is stored in the computer system. A database management system (DBMS) is an application that interacts with users, other applications and the database to collect, analyze and compute data for further use. This is where you store documents and other forms of data in the database.

(49) (C) 40.

The ratio of bottles to guests is 25 bottles: 50 guests.

When you simplify, it would be 1:2, or 0.5. This means that there will be 0.5 bottles available for every guest.

Since there is an increase of 30 guests, the total guests will be 30 + 50 = 80 guests.

Therefore, 0.5 × 80 guests = 40 bottles will be needed for 80 guests.

(50) (C) $300.

Ten percent is the same as 10/100. To get the percentage out of $3,000, multiply by 10/100. That is:

10/100 × $3,000.

When you divide $3,000 by 100 by canceling the zeros, you will have $30.

Then multiply $30 by 10, which is left in the calculation = $300.

Therefore, 10% of $3,000 is $300.

(51) (C) 45.

Take the constant term at the left side, +5, to the right-hand side (it changes to -5).

Therefore, we will have:

X = 50 − 5

X = 45

Another way of solving this equation is to eliminate both sides by 5 (to make X stand-alone). That is:

X + 5 − 5 = 50 − 5

X = 45.

(52) (B) 56.

Rearrange the numbers to follow this sequence:

25, 34, 43, 56, 67, 83, 90

Now, count from the left and right. You'll see that the median, or middle, value is 56.

The formula to solve for the median is:

n + 1 / 2, where n is the number of figures.

From the example above, n = 7

Therefore, 7 + 1 / 2 = 8/2

= 4

The fourth figure after organizing the numbers is the median. This makes 56 the median.

(53) (A) Land.

In economics, land is a natural resource that includes the earth's surface, the atmosphere (including the internet space), the water bodies and below the earth's surface. Land is a free gift of nature, and it is physically immobile. This is where all other factors of production take place.

(54) (C) Circulating assets.

Circulating capital is also called working capital. It is used to initiate production. It includes cash in hand, loans, overdrafts, shares and plowed-back profits. Circulating capital is, at times, called money capital. Capital is an asset that is set aside to facilitate the production process. There are two broad classifications of capital: fixed capital and circulating capital.

(55) (C) The law of diminishing returns.

This law states that when there is an increase in the utility of a factor of production (like labor) while other factors (like land) remain constant, then there will, first of all, be an increase in return of production, followed by a fall. It is sometimes regarded as the law of variable proportion or non-proportional returns.

(56) (B) Partnership.

A partnership comprises the resources of two to 20 individuals in the establishment and operations of the business. Each partner has a quota of profits they are allotted based on agreement. Depending on available collateral, the organization may take loans from banks. Partnerships are more stable and enjoy more continuity than sole proprietorships.

(57) (A) Demand.

In economics, demand is the quantity of goods and services consumers are willing and have the capacity to buy at a defined price and time. Demand is not always static. It is affected by factors such as the price of the goods and services, the price of complementary and competing goods and services, income, population size, changes in preferences of consumers, environmental and social conditions and government policies.

(58) (D) Derived.

When goods and services are demanded because of the demand for other products, it is called derived demand. There are five general classifications of demand: competitive demand, derived demand, complementary or joint demand, composite demand and independent demand. An example of derived demand is sugar and flour. They are needed because there is a need for baking.

(59) (A) Capitalism.

Capitalism is a market system that requires private control of properties. In a capitalist state, there is free enterprise, which is regulated by governmental agencies. Private owners have the freedom to explore opportunities within the capacity of their capital. A capitalist state is highly competitive, and the primary pursuit is to make a profit. The United States is a capitalist society.

(60) (A) Communist.

Communism is the culmination of socialism. It is idealistic in principle. Like socialism, all the means of production are owned by the community, which takes part in the income and the labor involved. Communism is theoretically a process that goes through four stages of social evolution (bourgeois capitalism, then dictatorship of the proletariat, which metamorphosizes into socialism and then communism).

Test 3: Situational Judgment Answers and Explanations

(61) (D) Identify those who are skilled in this area and divide the task into roles.

Henri Foyal believed that when work is divided into units, there will be greater productivity and quality of output. When there is an appropriate division of work, there is efficiency, speed and order. The number one rule in management is delegation. Tasks should be delegated to the best hands. Apply the rule of specialization so that everyone gets to do what they are passionate about and skilled at.

(62) (C) There should be room for questioning.

If there must be quality management, then a recognized authority must be in place. Everyone must know what their roles are in the department. The authorities must understand their responsibilities and execute them without reservations. There should be room for questioning for the purpose of clarity and redress on complex issues.

(63) (A) You will need discipline.

Discipline is an essential commodity in management. When there is no discipline, there will be no productivity. Discipline ensures that everyone does their job without unnecessary coercing or overbearing supervision. You must possess this quality if you plan to excel in the Foreign Service.

(64) (C) Avoid meddling in the matters of those who are not directly below them.

Every employee or Foreign Service officer should report to just one boss. A multiplicity of instructions from different bosses often results in confusion and conflict. This is called disunity in command. Therefore, authorities should not interfere with the affairs of employees who are not directly below them.

(65) (A) Specific.

Everyone in your department should be pursuing the same or similar goals. This is called unity of direction. The goals must be specific, measurable, attainable, relevant to making an impact in the US economy and time bound. That is why you should be aware of the decade, yearly, quarterly, monthly, weekly and daily goals of the current US administration and your department.

(66) (D) Your country's.

Foreign Service officers are referred to as civil servants because they are in the field to serve the United States. It is wrong and unconstitutional to put your interest above your nation's. Even if the situation benefits your nation of origin, you must forgo personal sentiments and work toward US goals.

(67) (D) All of the above.

Reward is a factor that should be considered in management. Rewards can be either financial or non-financial. It can be praise, recognition, a day off or any other means. When leading a team, never expect that your employees' passion for service is all they need to get the task done. Remuneration is a source of motivation.

(68) (A) A balanced approach to power-sharing.

Henri Fayol believed that the central body or management should maintain a neutral stance. He stated that a balanced approach to power-sharing is the best way to manage an organization. Power should not be top full and bottom empty, nor should it be the reverse. When power is distributed equally, there will be fluidity and progress.

(69) (D) Work without following the hierarchy of structure.

Fayol stipulates that a hierarchy should start from the top and flow to the bottom. Every officer should have direct access to their superiors. This chain is needed for the transfer of information, promotion of officers and specialization in roles.

(70) (D) Efficiency does not demand orderliness.

This is not true. When there is no orderliness, the new order will be frustration, lack of productivity and chaos. The workplace environment and atmosphere must be appropriate if efficiency is the sole goal. Seats, tables, decor and every aspect of the work environment should boost officer morale.

(71) (D) Should be treated with equity.

In the workplace, you should treat everyone with equity. There should be no racial, gender, religious or personal biases. No employee or customer should face discrimination. For example, it is common for some people to categorize all Muslims as terrorists and therefore treat individuals from this background with suspicions and prejudice. This is inappropriate.

(72) (A) Job security.

Employees tend to work better if there is stability in the workplace. If the administration offers job security, fewer penalties and an enabling environment, employees will feel safe to invest their time and effort. Administrators must give workers an assurance of their investment in labor through pensions, social welfare and less downsizing.

(73) (A) Initiative.

Initiative is the hallmark of exceptional Foreign Service officers. As a Foreign Service officer, you have to take an innovative approach toward problem-solving.

(74) (D) None of the above.

In the work arena, there should be trust, understanding and loyalty to the mission. Foreign Service officers must always put their nation first. To be productive, you will have to communicate and integrate with other Foreign Service officers who share the same values as you. Qualities such as envy, unhealthy competition and over-ambition should not be in the workplace.

(75) (A) Esprit de corps.

Esprit de corps is a feeling of oneness shared among members of the same group who are pursuing one goal. In the work arena, there should be trust, understanding and loyalty to the mission.

(76) (A) Monetary reward.

Motivation is a key factor in the workplace. Foreign Service officers who are motivated through monetary rewards or other forms of rewards tend to be more productive. Humans are wired to stake their time and efforts on things that will gratify them personally. Apply this rule when dealing with people as a diplomat. Do not be too quick to make your own interests obvious.

(77) (D) Try to ensure everyone goes home a winner.

If you allow the other party to see how they will benefit from a deal or negotiation, then everyone goes home a winner.

(78) (C) Respectfully tell your boss it's too much to handle.

Too much work will lead to a lack of productivity. Do not stress yourself or others. It is also unethical to outsource jobs to outsiders without your boss's consent. And quitting your job without addressing the problem is not appropriate.

(79) (B) Visit a counselor.

Your mental health is a priority in the workplace. It is best to address issues by seeking help. If you are having personal problems, visit a counselor.

(80) (C) The children.

When on a diplomatic mission and you have to choose, the children should come first, then the old. This is because these people cannot do certain things on their own. Also, remember that those with physical challenges, pregnancy and other difficulties can be given certain preferential treatments.

(81) (C) Do not relay sensitive, confidential information to her.

When dealing with sanguines, learn to be patient with them. Allow them to do most of the talking and listen attentively to what they are saying. They are more likely to follow you if you show that you understand their perception of things. However, be careful about how much confidential information you disclose to them because they are likely to share information with others.

(82) (C) Be practical when dissuading the officer.

Cholerics are very assertive with their decisions. They are quick in carrying out their plans and they are risk takers. Cholerics like to be in charge. Therefore, they do not mind making decisions for others, and this attitude makes them seem domineering.

(83) (D) All of the above.

Phlegmatics are often passive about life issues, even regarding things others seem to consider very important. They prefer to stick to what they are used to. You know that a colleague is phlegmatic if the person is calm, easygoing, ambivalent and ready to take instructions from others. The loyalty of a phlegmatic is not to be questioned.

(84) (C) Knowledgeable about your opinions.

When working with melancholics, be ready to share details of plans or activities. They expect you to be very knowledgeable about whatever you are telling them. Do not be in a hurry to get them to decide, because they will not do so until they have done their homework and are certain of their plans. Do not get annoyed when they pick out inconspicuous mistakes that are normally overlooked.

(85) (B) Four.

As you go about your job as a Foreign Service officer, be ready to work with people of different temperaments. There are basically four kinds of temperaments: sanguine, choleric, phlegmatic and melancholic.

(86) (A) Similar goals.

Everyone in your department should be pursuing same or similar goals. The goals must be specific, measurable, attainable, relevant to making an impact on the US economy and time bound.

(87) (A) The United States.

Foreign Service officers are referred to as civil servants because they are in the field to serve the United States. It is wrong and unconstitutional to put your interests above your nation. Even if the situation would benefit your nation of origin, you must forgo personal sentiments and work toward US goals.

(88) (D) All of the above.

Reward is a factor that should be considered in management. Rewards can be either financial or non-financial. It can be praise, recognition, a day off, etc.

Test 3: English Expressions Answers and Explanations

(89) (A) Often.

This is an adverb of frequency. An adverb modifies the action of a verb, the description of an adjective, or another adverb. Adverbs often end in *-ly*, *-wise*, or *-ward*. Examples are *slowly, happily, angrily, clockwise, backward*. Other examples of adverbs are *however, furthermore, very, only* and *since*.

(90) (D) Make the initial letter lowercase.

This is a common noun. It is not specific to a particular entity. Common nouns should not be capitalized.

(91) (A) Nothing.

Every aspect of the interrogative sentence is correct. Therefore, no aspect of the sentence should be edited or replaced.

(92) (D) The period.

The clauses need a comma. The comma is meant to ensure fluency in a text. It is used to separate sentences or ideas that depend on each other.

(93) (D) All of the above.

Norvig and Russell investigated four methods of characterizing AI technology. These are humane thinking, sane thinking, humane actions and reasonable actions. The first two categorizations make reference to thought, while the latter two focus on the conduct of AI technology. This categorization is a reference to every scientist who wishes to undertake the study and invention of intelligent machines.

(94) (B) I met a kind woman on my way from the examination.

This option is more concise than the other options. It briefly presents the message without altering the meaning. It is clear and unambiguous. Wordiness and redundancy should be avoided when writing standard English.

(95) (D) The buildings were demolished ten years ago, although we can still see some parts of them.

All the other answer options are not properly punctuated.

(96) (B) Oh! You have finally been employed in the Foreign Service department.

The exclamation mark is used to express joy, pain or surprise.

(97) (B) Which.

The phrase *which car was stolen* is in relation to Allen. This means that the phrase is telling us about Allen. This is sometimes called a WH-relative clause because it contains the relative pronoun *which*. Other relative pronouns are *who, that, whose, where, when,* etc. *Which* is used for non-living things. There may be a comma to separate the relative clause from the item that is being described.

(98) (A) No errors.

The subject in this statement is *The director general* and is singular. Therefore, the verb should be singular.

(99) (C) Was here.

When the lexical item *number of* is used and the statement starts with the definite article *the,* the verb should be singular. This shows that the writer is being specific.

However, it should be plural if the statement starts with the indefinite articles *a* or *an*. The indefinite article means that the subject is undefined or not specific. Therefore, the verb *were* should have been used.

(100) (C) Is.

The question is on pronoun case. The sentence requires the use of a possessive pronoun. Possessive pronouns are *his, her, its, my, mine, their, theirs, your, yours, our* and *ours*. They are used to show ownership. The lexical *is* is a verb and should not be used as a possessive.

(101) (C) Has been grazing.

This question is on concord. Concord is the agreement between grammatical items. According to the rule of concord, there are some plural nouns that look like singular nouns because they do not take the -s form. They should always be used with plural verbs. Examples include *cattle, clergy, people.*

(102) (A) 1, 2, 3, 4.

The correct order of the paragraph should read: (1) *The internet is an electronic network that allows millions of people across the globe to share information. (2) The internet has many advantages and disadvantages. (3) Some children watch violent and pornographic films on the internet. (4) Parents should offer guidance to their children.*

Sentence 1 contains the thesis statement and defines *the internet*. Sentence 2 should follow sentence 1 because it generally states the effect of the subject matter. Sentence 3 should come after sentence 2 because it supports the disadvantages of the internet. Sentence 4 should follow sentence 1 as the final paragraph because it provides a solution to the problem.

(103) (A) 2, 1, 4, 3.

The correct order of the paragraph should read: *(2) Unemployment is when there is unutilized labor that could have been engaged for productivity. (1) Many developing countries are facing the challenge of high unemployment. (4) There are various reasons for the increase in unemployment. (3) Another cause of unemployment is the abandonment of the economy's agricultural sector.*

Sentence 2 contains the thesis statement and defines *unemployment*. Sentence 1 should follow sentence 2 because it broadly highlights the effect of unemployment. Sentence 4 should come after sentence 1 because it supports the problem and causes of unemployment. Sentence 3 should follow sentence 4 because it begins with the transitional marker *another*, which shows that it is a continuation of sentence 4.

(104) (A) 1, 2, 3, 4.

The correct order of the paragraph should read: *(1) Bribery and corruption is the illegal offering of money or non-monetary valuables to influence the decision of someone in authority. (2) It is a social menace that can be found in public service. (3) Furthermore, bribery and corruption can be found in the educational sector. (4) There are opinions that bribery and corruption can be stopped in agencies, government and executives.*

Sentence 1 contains the thesis statement and defines *bribery and corruption*. Sentence 2 should follow sentence 1 because it broadly highlights the challenges of bribery and corruption. Sentence 3 should come after sentence 2 because it supports the problem and causes of bribery and corruption through the use of the transitional marker *furthermore*. Sentence 4 should follow sentence 3 because it provides a solution.

(105) (A) 2, 1, 4, 3.

The correct order of the paragraph should read: *(2) Most diseases are contagious; that is, they are communicable from one person to another. (1) Immunization is a way of preventing diseases by injecting specially treated disease-causing organisms into the body. (4) The terms vaccination and inoculation may be used to mean immunization. (3) Immunization usually begins from the days of pregnancy and shortly after birth.*

Sentence 2 contains the thesis statement. Sentence 1 should follow sentence 2 because it gives a narrower definition of the word *immunization*. Sentence 4 should come after sentence 1 because it further discusses the word *immunization*. Sentence 3 should follow sentence 4 because it is a continuation of the discussion of the word *immunization*.

(106) (D) 1, 3, 4, 2.

The correct order of the paragraph should read: *(1) Patriotism is how we show that we love our country and will be ready to serve it. (3) If Americans are called to serve their country in times of war or peace, they should be ready to serve. (4) As citizens of America, we should be loyal to our state and federal governments. (2) Being patriotic also means respecting national identity.*

Sentence 1 contains the thesis statement and defines *patriotism*. Sentence 3 should follow sentence 1 because it tells more about service to one's country. Sentence 4 should come after sentence 3 because it tells more about loyalty to one's country. Sentence 2 should follow sentence 4 because it adds more to the discussion of patriotism.

(107) (D) Sentence 4.

"Several scientists have postulated that HIV was a result of mistaken genetic engineering" should be added after, *"However, there are some grave danger of genetic engineering."*

The correct option is D because the omitted item, *"Several scientists have postulated that HIV was a result of mistaken genetic engineering,"* conveys that it is the continuation of Sentence 4.

(108) (A) Dangers.

The **incorrect** sentence is: *However, there are some grave danger of genetic engineering.*

Option A is the correct answer because the determiner (*some*) of the sentence is plural; therefore, the noun should take the plural form *dangers*. Option B is wrong because the lexical item is an adjective that is improperly modified. Option C is wrong because the plural determiner, *some*, should not take the singular noun *limitation*. Option D is wrong because the plural determiner *some* should not take the singular noun *disadvantage*.

(109) (B) Analyses.

The correct sentence should read: *The professor did several analyses on the topic.*

Analyses is the plural of *analysis*. The use of the determiner *several* indicates that it is plural. Other examples of nouns that take foreign forms to form their plurals are *basis - bases, phenomenon - phenomena, stratum - strata, stimulus - stimuli, criterion - criteria, oasis - oases, syllabus - syllabuses - syllabi, formula - formulas - formulae, memorandum - memorandums - memoranda*, etc.

(110) (C) On.

The correct sentence should read: *I dropped by <u>on</u> Wednesday.*

This is a question on prepositions. Prepositions are grammatical items that connect other grammatical items together. Examples are to, *in, on, with, across. On* is used for days of the week. For instance, *on Tuesday, on Saturday, on Monday.*

(111) (A) Have.

The correct sentence should read: *The girls <u>have</u> danced today.*

The verb *have* is plural. It is used with plural subjects. The only exception is the first-person singular personal pronouns *I* and *you*. Example: *We have talked to the man.* On the other hand, *I* and *you* can be used with the verb *have*. For instance, *I have seen the man. You have seen the lady.*

(112) (A) Are.

The correct sentence should read: *Jacob and Andrew <u>are fighting</u>.*

The verb *are* is plural. It is used for plural subjects. The subject in the sentence is a plural subject. This is known as grammatical concord.

(113) (C) In.

The correct sentence should read: *The man is <u>in</u> the office.*

The preposition *in* is used to show the position of an object or thing. It is used to highlight the inner part of something or being a participant in something.

(114) (C) Is.

The correct sentence should read: *Gymnastics is my favorite sport.*

This falls under the grammatical concord rule. Concord is the agreement between grammatical items. There are some nouns that end in -s but are not plural. Instead, they are singular. Since they are singular, they are to be followed by singular verbs. Examples of singular nouns that end in -s include *mathematics* and *politics*.

(115) (A) Have.

The correct sentence should read: *The passengers, along with the bus driver, have been kidnapped.*

The first subject is the focus of the sentence. In the sentence, the first subject is *The passengers* and it is plural. Therefore, the plural verb *have* is appropriate.

(116) (B) Is.

The correct sentence should read: *Singing is a nice activity.*

This question is on concord. The subject is a singular subject. It is a gerund. Since it is a singular subject, a singular verb is expected to appear after it.

(117) (C) Were.

The correct sentence should read: *The women who came here were helped by the commissioner.*

Whenever a relative pronoun appears after a noun or a pronoun (nominal), the noun, pronoun or nominal determines the verb to be used. This means that if the key word is in the plural form, the verb will be plural too.

(118) (A) Is.

The correct sentence should read: *That man who is standing there is my teacher*

The key word is *man*. A singular verb (*is*) is used because *man* is a singular noun. Whenever a relative pronoun appears after a noun or a pronoun (nominal), the noun, pronoun, or nominal determines the verb to be used.

(119) (A) Have.

The correct sentence should read: *The kidnappers have been arrested.*

The kidnappers is the key word. Since it is in the plural form, the verb must also be in the plural form. *Have* is a plural form, while *has* is singular.

(120) (C) Us.

The correct sentence should read: *He gave us the book.*

The pronoun *us* is an object pronoun. Object pronouns appear after transitive verbs. It is wrong to place them before the transitive verb. If you intend to place pronouns before the transitive verb, you should use subject pronouns. Examples of object pronouns include *me, you, it, them, him, her.*

(121) (A) Theirs.

The correct sentence should read: *That book is theirs.*

This question is on pronouns. Pronouns are used in place of nouns to avoid repetition of nouns in a statement. *Theirs* is a plural possessive pronoun. It is used to show that something belongs to more than one person. Another example of a plural possessive pronoun is *ours*. For example, *That book is ours.*

(122) (B) The book is mine.

Mine is a personal possessive pronoun. It is used to show that something belongs to one person. It appears after a copular verb. It means that you own a possession.

(123) (D) Across.

The correct sentence should read: *I ran <u>across</u> the road.*

Across is a preposition that is used when moving from one place to another or when something is over a plane.

(124) (B) Is.

The correct sentence should read: *To be a good man <u>is</u> not easy.*

The subject is a singular subject. *To be a man* is a noun phrase. It is a single subject. It is a *to* infinitive and since it is a singular subject, a singular verb is used after it.

(125) (A) Yours.

The correct sentence should read: <u>*Yours*</u> *faithfully is a complimentary close used in a formal letter.*

Yours is a possessive pronoun that shows ownership. There is a difference between *yours* and *you're*. *You're* is a contracted form of *you are*. In writing formal letters, it is *Yours,* which is appropriate. A comma should not appear after the word.

(126) (A) Go.

The correct sentence should read: *My friends go to the cinema every weekend.*

The verb *go* is correct. The subject is a plural subject and as such, the verb should be plural.

(127) (D) Is.

The correct sentence should read: *Phonetics and phonology are difficult to study.*

The two subjects are regarded as one, so a singular verb is to be used. Other examples of singular subjects include *bow and arrow, bread and butter* and *chicken and rice.* These kinds of subjects are often complementary in nature. That is, they work together.

(128) (A) Is.

The correct sentence should read: *The commissioner of education, in the company of some principals, is carrying out inspections on schools.*

The commissioner of education is the key word. It is the subject that determines the verb. It is a singular subject, and the verb will be singular.

(129) (C) Is.

The correct sentence should read: *The number of school principals in the country is one hundred.*

When *a number of* comes before a noun, it is followed by a plural noun and the verb should be a plural verb. However, if it is *the number of*, it is followed by a plural noun but a singular verb. For example, *A number of people have agreed to the suggestion*. To erase doubts, simply remove *a number of* then only *students* is remaining. It becomes *students have arrived*.

(130) (A) Are.

The correct sentence should read: *Either the principal or the teachers are in school by now*.

This is the proximity concord rule. If two subjects are joined with *neither ... nor* or *either ... or*, the last subject before the verb will determine whether the verb will be singular or plural. *Teachers* is the closest subject to the verb and it is a plural noun or subject. It takes a plural verb.

(131) (C) Me.

The correct sentence should read: *The kind man helped Kola and me.*

The sentence has a transitive verb (*helped*). An object pronoun comes after a transitive verb. *Me* is an object pronoun, as is *us, her, them* and *him*. A subject pronoun cannot appear after a transitive verb, but it is possible for a subject pronoun to appear after a copular or intensive verb. It is correct to say *I am he* and *I am she*. But it is wrong to say *I am him*.

(132) (C) I.

The correct sentence should read: *My father and I saw the fight that took place in the market*.

I is a subject pronoun. It appears before a transitive verb. If *My father* is removed from the sentence, we are left with *I saw the fight that took place in the market*. The sentence is still correct because *I* is still in the subjective. A subject pronoun should not appear after a transitive verb.

(133) (B) Makes.

The correct sentence should read: Reading the Bible <u>makes</u> one grow spiritually.

Gerunds are noun phrases. It is a single subject (singular) and is to be followed by a singular verb. *-s* forms of verbs are singular.

(134) (D) It.

The correct sentence should read: *I gave you a ruler yesterday. You broke <u>it.</u>*

It is a pronoun. It is used for non-living things and animals. *Ruler* is a non-living thing and as such, the pronoun *it* is used.

(135) (A) It's.

The correct sentence should read: *<u>It's</u> high time we left this place.*

It's is a contracted form of *it is*. *It's* is different from *its* because the latter is a possessive pronoun that shows ownership and should take a preceding and modified noun.

(136) (B) Seen.

The correct sentence should read: *I have <u>seen</u> the book.*

The verb *seen* is in the past participle form. Whenever the verb *have* appears before a lexical verb, the lexical verb must be in the past participle form unless the lexical verb has the same past tense and past participle. For example, *called, carried, danced.*

(137) (A) Promised.

The correct sentence should read: *Last week, he had <u>promised</u> to help us.*

There is the verb *have* (*had*) before the lexical verb. As a result, the lexical verb must be in its past participle form. The verb *promise* has four forms because the past tense and the past participle forms are the same.

(138) (B) Are.

The correct sentence should read: *The clergy <u>are</u> here.*

The noun *clergy* is a plural noun like *people*. They look like singular nouns, but they are not. Whenever they are used, plural verbs go with them. For instance: *The people are happy*; *The clergy were here.*

(139) (B) The one who is very sure of what he is saying.

If you are ambivalent or disinterested in the information you are imparting to your audience, it will show in how energetically you communicate. People will believe almost anything as long as the speaker is sincerely passionate about the information.

(140) (D) You must be totally convinced that it is right.

Before you speak on foreign policy as a US delegate, you must have studied the policy, understand it and be totally convinced that it is right. As a Foreign Service officer, you have to be passionate about your country and its core values. You can be dogged in defending the name and policies of your country only if you are passionate about its fundamental ideologies.

(141) (D) Passion for your country.

Passion is what will make you, as a Foreign Service officer, ready to fight for your country. It is what will make you go to any lengths to speak in favor of US foreign policies.

(142) (C) They do not have long attention spans.

Audience members often do not have long attention spans, and their minds may wander off no matter how entertaining the session may be. Therefore, effective speakers are straightforward. They get straight to the point. Effective speakers know where to begin their presentation and when to stop.

(143) (D) Divide your speech into segments and give room for the audience to participate, contribute and ask questions.

Thirty minutes is a very long time to communicate with someone. If you speak too long, it will become boring. Divide your speech into parts and give room for the audience to participate, contribute and ask questions.

(144) (C) They are less likely to give their attention to something else.

When your audience is involved in the communication process, they are less likely to get distracted.

(145) (D) It may make your audience forget the key points you are trying to impart.

Wordiness may make your audience forget the key points you are trying to get across to them. Being succinct keeps the key points fresh in their minds.

(146) (C) Entertainment.

Humans seek to be entertained and enjoy themselves. Interesting stories keep an audience's attention. That is why storytelling is a magnetic ingredient that compels people to communicate.

(147) (B) Give listeners the pleasure of hearing a story.

Interesting stories keep an audience's attention.

(148) (C) It helps people retain information.

As a Foreign Service officer, you should know how to tell stories, be it fiction or nonfiction, when communicating. Make your story contextual and something your audience can relate to. This makes the information more vivid.

(149) (D) Environmental consciousness.

Effective speakers always desire to understand the audience. They want to know their sociocultural background, political views, religious beliefs and other characteristics.

(150) (D) All of the above.

If you are sent to be an ambassador in a foreign nation, you should study about the people you will be relating with. Read up about other people's experiences there. Look for a friendly local who can give you a head's up on what you should expect. Try to know what they do and who they are.

(151) (D) All of the above.

Be conscious of the time, atmosphere and place setting of where you are. An environment filled with noise and disorderliness will distort the flow of communication. Understand that every conversation has its own suitable environment. If the discussion will contain exclusive information that should be unknown to the public, then find a private place to communicate. The time of discussion also matters. Avoid discussing heavy matters in the evening or at night.

(152) (D) Not listing your key points.

Effective communication involves planning what you are going to say in your mind, verbally or as written notes before the presentation. You may want to list the key points that will serve as a reminder when speaking. This approach will help you be succinct. Highlight the purpose of the discussion. If it is a one-way speech, be direct with your points. Use repetition solely for emphasis.

(153) (A) Be clear with your articulation.

When giving a public speech to a group of people, you may want to begin with an anecdote. Also, be clear with your articulation. Remember to enunciate your words clearly. The volume of your voice should be audible for all to hear. The tone of your voice ought to be steady. You may want to increase your pitch and repeat the lines when reiterating key points.

Test 3: Essay Answer

Corrupt Public Officers Also Deserve Capital Punishment

Corruption is eating at our society like a cankerworm. It has penetrated almost every sector of American society. It is either overt or covert. In this essay, I will be highlighting key reasons why public officers should not be exempt from capital punishment when caught in corrupt practices.

Capital punishment is the highest punishment given to offenders of the law. It is the death penalty. This can be through electrocution, hanging, lethal injection, execution by firing squad and other lawful means. Some argue corruption is a lesser evil compared to the crimes that call for capital punishment. They forget that the victim of the crime of corruption is not just an individual, but a generation that is deprived of access to rightful wealth, infrastructure and other provisions society should give them. So, if murderers face capital punishment, public officers should not be left out.

Another reason public officers should face capital punishment is that they impoverish the masses. They siphon funds meant for public use and convert them for personal gains. What is meant to enrich the welfare of millions is diverted for a few tens or hundreds who benefit from the dividends of their fraudulent acts. When public officers plunder the economy of America, everything dies—often slowly—including the health sector, the schools, the financial institutions and policies.

Most foreigners see America as a country where corruption does not exist in public offices. However, this glittering image of America is becoming tarnished as the rate of corruption in the system continues to rise. It may get to the point where America will lose its position as a model that countries on every continent of the world should imitate. Our prima facie may get so deteriorated that it might affect international trade with other countries that want to trade with countries they can trust. If the drastic step of capital punishment is not taken, we can be sure that more corrupt officers will arise and upset the fulcrum on which the glory and prosperity of America are currently standing.

Another key area that establishes the fact that these fraudsters hiding under the auspices of white-collar jobs should receive capital punishment is that when they plunder the economy or tarnish the image of the country, investors will develop cold feet for rewarding opportunities they have found in our resourceful country. No entrepreneur wants to invest in a land whose government has been infested with corrupt public officers who will frustrate their investment plans. Americans cannot deny the fact that we need capital and human resources to keep propelling our nation as the foremost nation in the world.

Finally, capital punishment is the surest punitive measure that will serve as a deterrent to criminal public officers who plunder the nation's economy. Capital punishment will help our country stay as the model for all other countries, and it will revive the economic buoyancy of America.

CPSIA information can be obtained
at www.ICGtesting.com
Printed in the USA
BVHW091948171222
654415BV00009B/971

9 781989 726884